A CHOICE OF
WILLIAM MORRIS'S VERSE

A CHOICE OF WILLIAM MORRIS'S VERSE

selected
with an introduction by
GEOFFREY GRIGSON

FABER AND FABER
24 Russell Square
London

First published in 1969
by Faber and Faber Limited
24 Russell Square London W.C.1
Printed in Great Britain
by R. MacLehose and Company Limited
The University Press Glasgow
All rights reserved
Introduction © Geoffrey Grigson 1969

Standard Book No: [hard bound edition]
571 08400 1

Standard Book No: [edition in paper covers]
571 08980 1

Contents

William Morris

Born Elm House, Walthamstow, March 24, 1834. Lives at Woodford Hall, Essex, 1840–1847; at Water House, Walthamstow, from 1848. Marlborough College, Wiltshire, 1848–1851. Exeter College, Oxford, 1853–1855. *The Defence of Guenevere, and Other Poems*, 1858. Marries Jane Burden, daughter of an Oxford groom, 1859. Builds the Red House, Upton, Kent, 1859–1860, and lives there 1860–1865. Establishes the craft firm of Morris, Marshall, Faulkner and Co., 1861. *The Life and Death of Jason*, 1867. *The Earthly Paradise*, 1868–1870. Leases Kelmscott Manor, on the Upper Thames, 1871. Visits Iceland for the first time, 1871. *The Story of Sigurd the Volsung and the Fall of the Niblungs*, 1876. *Hopes and Fears for Art*, 1882. Joins the Democratic Federation, 1883. Edits and contributes to *The Commonweal*, journal of the Socialist League, 1885–1890. *The Pilgrims of Hope*, 1886. *A Dream of John Ball* and *Signs of Change*, 1888. Founds the Kelmscott Press, 1890. *News from Nowhere, or an Epoch of Rest*, 1891. *Poems by the Way*, 1891. *The Well at the World's End*, 1896. Dies at the age of sixty-two, October 3, 1896, and is buried in Kelmscott churchyard.

There is no complete edition of Morris's poems (his manuscripts are in the British Museum), editors having been deterred no doubt by their bulk. The greater part will be found in the *Collected Works*, edited in 24 volumes by his daughter May Morris, 1910–1965.

Introduction

Landing at Le Havre from a late car ferry an Englishman of to-day could do worse than think of William Morris, aged twenty-two, walking the quays there at night in the August of 1855. Waiting with him for a boat back to England was Ned Jones, and after a last term together at Oxford, and an exhilarating tour of French cathedrals, it was there, so we are told in Mackail's biography of Morris, that they came to the decision by which one of them was to be transformed into the now more or less disregarded, if not forgotten painter Sir Edward Burne-Jones, and the other — without title or double-barrelled name — into one of the seminal idealists of the nineteenth century: they decided on the quay to forgo the idea of becoming clergymen and to become instead devotees of the practice of art.

Art was at once the root and the leaf of Morris's idealism and of all that career of enormous activity which so helped to sweeten the English mind and make the English readier to accept and promote a society of greater happiness and justice; and Morris's primal art was the one we are inclined to dismiss or push out to the margin nowadays when we celebrate the energizer, the designer, the craftsman, the aesthete, and the communist.

That night at Le Havre, it is true, the young Morris had the making of buildings, not the writing of poems in mind. Thinking of the cathedrals he had just seen, the height of Beauvais, the opulence of Rouen, the purity of Coutances, it was to architecture that he decided to give himself, and architecture which he was trying before long under G. E. Street, only to abandon it for painting under the influence of his friend Rossetti. But he was already aware that he could write poems. After his trial excursions into architecture and painting his first book — and his best if we except *News from Nowhere* — was poetry, published in 1858, when Morris was twenty-four; and poems he was to continue to write, enshrining, if not always obviously, those hopes for mankind which he elaborated and expressed in so many other ways, poems short, medium, long or immoderately long, until his death in 1896.

That first book of his, *The Defence of Guenevere*, already displays in poem after poem the leit-motiv of Morris's thought and action, though it is too easily, and too frequently, dismissed as a backward ramble into day-dreams and mock-medievalism.

> There were four of us about that bed;
> The mass-priest knelt at the side,
> I and his mother stood at the head,
> Over his feet lay the bride;
> We were quite sure that he was dead,
> Though his eyes were open wide.

Such is the opening, direct and immediate under the influence of Browning, of one of these early poems, 'Shameful Death' (page 63). A young lord is murdered, the circumstances are described, the narrator is glad to recall, at seventy, how the two murderers, Sir John the knight of the Fen and Sir Guy of the Dolorous Blast, were caught up with and killed in their turn.

If it is read too casually, enjoyed too casually, 'Shameful Death' may be taken as no more than a poem of revenge or a story of rough justice. Yet it is an embryo of Morris's concern. In a shameful way men who are evil and cowardly come up behind the young Lord Hugh and catch him and hang him:

> He did not die in the night,
> He did not die in the day,
> But in the morning twilight
> His spirit pass'd away,
> When neither sun nor moon was bright,
> And the trees were merely grey.
>
> He was not slain with the sword,
> Knight's axe, or the knightly spear,
> Yet spoke he never a word
> After he came in here;
> I cut away the cord
> From the neck of my brother dear.

10

This shameful death has been inflicted (and in Morris there is no sick aestheticism, no indulgence in death or its details, no sado-masochism as there is so frequently in Rossetti or Swinburne) on a man young and brave and good, newly married and happy and in love.

> They lighted a great torch then,
>   When his arms were pinion'd fast,
> Sir John the knight of the Fen,
>   Sir Guy of the Dolorous Blast,
> With knights threescore and ten,
>   Hung brave Lord Hugh at last.

Happiness has been wilfully destroyed. For Morris, in love with the hills of earth, and no believer in a heavenly paradise, that was the cardinal sin, the cardinal pathos. His concern — in his poems and in all of his roles — was happiness, his regret that so many had so little chance to be happy, and that love and happiness, those twins, so much to be desired —

> To what a heaven the earth might grow
> If fear beneath the earth were laid,
> If hope failed not, nor love decayed

— are yet so vulnerable. His hatred — and Morris was explosive as well as placid — was for those who fight evilly against the actual and possible happiness of mankind:

> I am threescore and ten,
>   And my hair is all turn'd grey,
> But I met Sir John of the Fen
>   Long ago on a summer day,
> And am glad to think of the moment when
>   I took his life away.
>
> I am threescore and ten,
>   And my strength is mostly pass'd,
> But long ago I and my men,
>   When the sky was overcast,
> And the smoke roll'd over the reeds of the fen,
>   Slew Guy of the Dolorous Blast.

Critics have understood that Morris's concern for happiness was not a contemptible motivation. Yeats, for example; who knew him face to face, and wrote of him with perfect lack of superiority in his paper 'The Happiest of Poets'. Yeats was well aware of the limitation of his verse and his vision, yet declared with approval that he made his poetry 'out of unending pictures of a happiness that is often what a child might imagine, and always a happiness that sets mind and body at ease'; in which he was 'unlike all other modern writers'. Readers had been taught 'to sympathize with the unhappy until they had grown morbid', Morris's work was to make them sympathize 'with men and women who turned everything into happiness' because they contained some of the fullness of natural life. Yeats's elaboration and celebration of the happiness which was Morris's concern, could not be more generous. Yet it is curious that he leaves one to think of Morris — others have done the same with less sympathy — as a poet without the complementary words of sadness or regret. He had just quoted the exquisite opening of 'Golden Wings' (also in Morris's first book of 1858):

> Midways of a walled garden,
>   In the happy poplar land,
>   Did an ancient castle stand,
> With an old knight for a warden.
>
> Many scarlet bricks there were
>   In its walls, and old grey stone;
>   Over which red apples shone
> At the right time of the year.
>
> On the bricks the green moss grew,
>   Yellow lichen on the stone,
>   Over which red apples shone;
> Little war that castle knew.

'The verses,' Yeats said, 'ran in my head for years and became to me the best description of happiness in the world, and I am not certain that I know a better even now.' The poem changes.

> The water slips,
> The red-bill'd moorhen dips.
> Sweet kisses on red lips;

> Alas! the red rust grips.
> And the blood-red dagger rips ...

> White swans on the green moat,
> Small feathers left afloat
> By the blue-painted boat;
> Swift running of the stoat.

And with the stoat of shameful death coming to men and women who deserve better, I wonder why Yeats made no mention of apples now 'green and sour' and the moat, which had been transformed:

> The draggled swans most eagerly eat
> The green weeds trailing in the moat;
> Inside the rotting leaky boat
> You see a slain man's stiffened feet.

So it is in poem after poem: Sir Peter Harpdon shows reluctant mercy and lives to be hanged ('Sir Peter Harpdon's End', page 31). The knight and his lady were killed, and the girl's white skull was found with her gold tresses inside the coif of the helmet which he had taken off and made her wear for her own safety ('Concerning Geffray Teste Noire', page 58). In 'The Blue Closet' (page 67), in which one sees the strangest and most credible of the Pre-Raphaelite or post-pre-Raphaelite lilies —

> Through the floor shot up a lily red,
> With a patch of earth from the land of the dead,
> For he was strong in the land of the dead

— death extinguishes the last vestiges of happiness and love:

> And ever the great bell overhead,
> And the tumbling seas mourned for the dead;
> For their song ceased, and they were dead.

In 'The Haystack in the Floods' (page 77) —

> Had she come all the way for this,
> To part at last without a kiss?

13

Yea, had she borne the dirt and rain
That her own eyes might see him slain
Beside the haystack in the floods?

In 'Helen Arming Paris' (page 86), one of the *Scenes from the Fall of Troy*, which Morris was writing between 1861 and 1866, when he began *The Earthly Paradise* (they were never finished, and never published in his lifetime), Helen wildly imagines his death and her return to Greece, happiness over; and when Morris (but less surely) emerges from that distancing which so often helps in rounding off and establishing a poem, and writes in *The Pilgrims of Hope*, twenty years later, about the Commune and the fighting in Paris —

So at last from a grey stone building we saw a great flag fly,
One colour, red and solemn 'gainst the blue of the spring-tide sky

— the 'new proletarian' of the poem loses his wife's love, and then his wife and his friend, whom she loved, on the barricades.

Reverting to 'Shameful Death', it is a poem which exemplifies other things creditable to Morris. One is Morris's power to actualize his dream-world or its defeat. Projecting that world into the past or into the future of *News from Nowhere*, Morris was able to feel it and to present it in the here and now of preferred environments; and when he does so, his language avoids archaism or verbal costume or the artificial silk common in too much of the mid or late 19th century manner (compare the poetry language, unattached to earth or Earthly Paradise, of Morris's friend Rossetti, or the poetry language of those elongate figures so infinitely repeated by his friend Burne-Jones). Environmentally one thinks of Morris in his poems, or most of them, and in his calm and cool designs, as the socialist lord of Kelmscott along the Thames; but it was not until 1871 that he acquired Kelmscott as a country resort; in his earlier poems, so clear-cut, so economical, so direct in language, the young Morris is still only the proprietor, so to say, of the landscapes and properties of childhood. When he was six the wealthy Morris family had moved from Walthamstow (his birth place — he had narrowly escaped birth in Lombard Street, in the heart of profit and capital) to Woodford Hall, which was his home until his father's death in 1847. There was a private park attached to the hall; and beyond the fence of these fifty acres of a first happiness there stretched, ad infinitum, as it must have seemed, the pollarded hornbeams and the bracken of Epping Forest, the gnarled growth and undergrowth of murder — and of 'A Shameful Death':

> He did not strike one blow,
> For the recreants came behind,
> In a place where the hornbeams grow,
> A path right hard to find,
> For the hornbeam boughs swing so,
> That the twilight makes it blind.

I would see the fringes of Epping Forest too — hazels for horn-beams — in the Verville wood entered in the poem about Geffray Teste Noire, the Gascon knight and thief:

> And so we enter'd Verville wood next day

> In the afternoon; through it the highway runs,
> 'Twixt copses of green hazel, very thick,
> And underneath, with glimmering of suns,
> The primroses are happy; the dews lick

> The soft green moss. . . .

The third home the Morrises came to occupy when his father died, gave him the happy and less happy moated actuality of 'Golden Wings'.

Morris's socialism demanded more than the private park or grounds; so it was around Kelmscott Manor, which became the symbol of his dream, his career and his personality, that Morris envisioned his *News from Nowhere*, his 'Epoch of Rest', his account of England in ideal content after revolution. He walked out of the garden wicket of Kelmscott Manor, and the ideal state of the future, or the medieval ideal of the folk-mote, was the practical actual hay meadow, was the long unhedged open fields by the summer flow of the Thames, was the enjoyed flow, placidity, purity, and mirror-surface of the Thames, broken only by oars, or bleak, or chubb, that upper Thames which is also William Morris, under willows and past its tall water flowers of yellow or rose-pink or reverberating purple. The river landscape makes the language and cadence of the happy prose in *News from Nowhere*, which has a quality of the light of five a.m., and of many happy if regretful stanzas which were to be collected in *Poems by the Way* (1891). The elements — as a mild wind turns the willow leaves — which make the measured humanized external environment so pleasant, whatever the blemishes of the day such as the pinched faces of ill-fed haymakers under their flapping sun-bonnets, should extend again, Morris pleads, into the nature of man, and into his ecological circumstance. So, among the various elements of the medieval, should that craftsman's state of mind which without question had raised the church spires and bell-turrets above the horizons of that happy river-land ('The chancel . . . was so new that the dust of the stone still lay white on the midsummer grass beneath the carvings of the windows'. *The Dream of John Ball*, Chapter I).

If men went out to a war of arrows and axes in defence of their dignity as men, it was the shorn hayfields and stubbles of contentment they crossed in such poems as 'The Burghers' Battle' (page 127) or 'The Folk-mote by the River'. And it was the Thames, twisting through Morris's thought and emotion, which eventually widened past 'the high tower of the Parliament House, or Dung Market' (which it had become by the time of *News from Nowhere*) into all the rest of the filth of the civilization he repudiated, below the burrows of the deprived whom *The Times* spoke of so contemptuously, between inverted commas, as the 'unemployed'.

Contentment finds an autumnal apogee (Morris is a good hand at the stillness of autumn) in a poem of slow movement which comes in the middle of *The Story of the Glittering Plain*, one of the prose romances Morris wrote in his last years (and printed in his Golden Type at his Kelmscott Press):

> Dumb is the hedge where the crabs hang yellow,
> Bright as the blossoms of the spring;
> Dumb is the close where the pears grow mellow,
> And none but the dauntless redbreasts sing . . .
>
> Come then, love, for peace is upon us,
> Far off is failing, and far is fear,
> Here where the rest in the end hath won us,
> In the garnering tide of the happy year.

Come from the grey old house by the water,
Where, far from the lips of the hungry sea,
Green groweth the grass o'er the field of the slaughter,
And all is a tale for thee and me.

Certainly it conveys Kelmscott by the Thames, the ideal within the worldly, and the lapse of existence. But do such cadences and such a predilection convict Morris, in a fatal sense, of superficiality?

Superficial belongs to Class One of pejorative words, though surface matters are not *ipso facto* denied either a human relevance or fine qualities which give pleasure; and poetry is of many kinds; and we should avoid superiority when faced with a kind which no one could or would write in our own day, when we have found it so difficult to share Morris's 'reverence for the life of Man upon the Earth'. It is true that in his thirties Morris began to lose the passion and so the directness of his verse. The reasons seem partly in the pressure of his relentless activities as designer and manufacturer, partly in Morris's own nature, and partly in the discovery of the nature of his wife, who may or may not have transferred her affections — if she had affections at all? — to Rossetti,* coupled with a possible realization that the quality of love which *might* have come from a wife of such matchless stupidity as well as such matchless beauty could not in any case have been very satisfying. Certainly with and after *The Life and Death of Jason* (1867) and the unpressurized tales of *The Earthly Paradise* (1868–1870) Morris takes language and makes it flow and flow. Certainly he gave way to an increasing archaism, certainly his lines elongate across the page into a tom-tom rhythm which deadens the reader's attention (true notably of the epic *Story of Sigurd the Volsung*, in spite of its intermittent power). And then in the eighties Morris separated his idea from its expression in poetry, fabrics, wall-papers and the rest, brandished it naked, and became an active propagator of revolutionary socialism. He can be wearisome, as Yeats remarked so equably — 'His poetry often wearies us as the unbroken green

* Read the tortured confessional poems of the late sixties, 'Thunder in the Garden', 'Sad-eyed and Soft and Grey', 'Rhyme Slayeth Shame', 'May Grown A-cold', 'Song', 'Why Dost Thou Struggle', 'Fair Weather and Foul', and the September lines from *The Earthly Paradise*.

of July wearies us.' What has so often been called his tapestry verse, even at its happiest in *The Earthly Paradise*, hardly bears reprinting ('They are all too long and flabby, damn it !' — Morris to Swinburne on the tales in *The Earthly Paradise*). His socialist hymnology is mostly water off the boil, useful, but not poetry. I shall speak up, all the same, for the long unfinished poem *The Pilgrims of Hope* (a portion will be found on pages 135–138), which Morris contributed with so much urgent political writing to *The Commonweal*, the journal he edited for the Socialist League. Also for 'A Death Song' (page 139), one of those poems with a refrain which Morris managed so well. With thirty-two years between them, thirty-two years of a life of astonishing creativity, it recalls a scene which may be set alongside that midnight pacing on the quay at Le Havre. Morris wrote it in 1887 for the funeral of Alfred Linnell who died of a broken hip some weeks after the trouble between police and demonstrators over the right to meet and speak in Trafalgar Square. Rightly or wrongly the police were blamed for his death. 'Killed in Trafalgar Square' was emblazoned above the hearse which took Linnell in a long ragged procession from Soho to Bow Cemetery. It was then the dark of a December evening, and in a cold rain which had driven away most of the crowd, Morris and a few others chanted the Death Song above Linnell's grave.*

Omitting most of the tapestry (and most of Morris's explicitly socialist versifying) amounts to a drastic reduction. Nevertheless it leaves a body of poems now undervalued which would still be this man's title to a just remembrance, even if nothing else of him were known.

Yeats, who had watched Morris holding a glass of claret to the light and exclaiming that wine was no prosaic source of inspiration since the grapes which made the wine were themselves made by sap and sunlight, declared that we are a little happier when we look at his vision. So we are. It is as if Morris had wished, and then worked, to share the happiness of his own childhood with all of

---

* A peculiarly vigorous and moving, if prejudiced account of the procession, of Morris and other organizers following the hearse, and of the chanting in the cemetery will be found in *The Times*, for December 19th, 1887.

the deprived, as if he had hoped that the happiness of childhood could be prolonged, and extended into the rest of life, into everyone's life, untarnished by the disappointments of love and refreshed by that excellence of the earth which Morris loved with such poignancy. If he has been slighted lately as a poet, isn't it — for one thing — because we have been slighting the earth he celebrated, the only earth, the only life, we have, more than our disasters and discontents have warranted?

Towards the end he too believed that the arts had become unreal in his time. 'The arts have got to die, what is left of them, before they can be born again.' 'Nothing can take serious hold of people, or should do so, but that which is rooted deepest in reality and is quite at first hand: there is no room for anything which is not forced out of a man of deep feeling, because of its innate strength and vision.' So he was severe on his own verse as on his own life; more severe than we need be, who can look back, and compare, and see the realities and honesties of either one.

GEOFFREY GRIGSON

The Defence of Guenevere

But, knowing now that they would have her speak,
She threw her wet hair backward from her brow,
Her hand close to her mouth touching her cheek,

As though she had had there a shameful blow,
And feeling it shameful to feel ought but shame
All through her heart, yet felt her cheek burned so,

She must a little touch it ; like one lame
She walked away from Gauwaine, with her head
Still lifted up ; and on her cheek of flame

The tears dried quick ; she stopped at last and said :
'O knights and lords, it seems but little skill
To talk of well-known things past now and dead.

'God wot I ought to say, I have done ill,
And pray you all forgiveness heartily !
Because you must be right such great lords — still

'Listen, suppose your time were come to die,
And you were quite alone and very weak ;
Yea, laid a dying while very mightily

'The wind was ruffling up the narrow streak
Of river through your broad lands running well :
Suppose a hush should come, then some one speak :

' "One of these cloths is heaven, and one is hell,
Now choose one cloth for ever, which they be,
I will not tell you, you must somehow tell

' "Of your own strength and mightiness ; here, see !"
Yea, yea, my lord, and you to ope your eyes,
At foot of your familiar bed to see

'A great God's angel standing, with such dyes,
Not known on earth, on his great wings, and hands,
Held out two ways, light from the inner skies

'Showing him well, and making his commands
Seem to be God's commands, moreover, too,
Holding within his hands the cloths on wands;

'And one of these strange choosing cloths was blue,
Wavy and long, and one cut short and red;
No man could tell the better of the two.

'After a shivering half-hour you said,
"God help! heaven's colour, the blue;" and he said, "hell."
Perhaps you then would roll upon your bed,

'And cry to all good men that loved you well,
"Ah Christ! if only I had known, known, known;"
Launcelot went away, then I could tell,

'Like wisest man how all things would be, moan,
And roll and hurt myself, and long to die,
And yet fear much to die for what was sown.

'Nevertheless you, O Sir Gauwaine, lie,
Whatever may have happened through these years,
God knows I speak truth, saying that you lie.'

Her voice was low at first, being full of tears,
But as it cleared, it grew full loud and shrill,
Growing a windy shriek in all men's ears,

A ringing in their startled brains, until
She said that Gauwaine lied, then her voice sunk,
And her great eyes began again to fill,

Though still she tood right up, and never shrunk,
But spoke on bravely, glorious lady fair!
Whatever tears her full lips may have drunk,

She stood, and seemed to think, and wrung her hair,
Spoke out at last with no more trace of shame,
With passionate twisting of her body there:

'It chanced upon a day that Launcelot came
To dwell at Arthur's court: at Christmas-time
This happened; when the heralds sung his name,

' "Son of King Ban of Benwick," seemed to chime
Along with all the bells that rang that day,
O'er the white roofs, with little change of rhyme.

'Christmas and whitened winter passed away,
And over me the April sunshine came,
Made very awful with black hail-clouds, yea

'And in the Summer I grew white with flame,
And bowed my head down — Autumn, and the sick
Sure knowledge things would never be the same,

'However often Spring might be most thick
Of blossoms and buds, smote on me, and I grew
Careless of most things, let the clock tick, tick,

'To my unhappy pulse, that beat right through
My eager body; while I laughed out loud,
And let my lips curl up at false or true,

'Seemed cold and shallow without any cloud.
Behold my judges, then the cloths were brought:
While I was dizzied thus, old thoughts would crowd,

'Belonging to the time ere I was bought
By Arthur's great name and his little love,
Must I give up for ever then, I thought,

'That which I deemed would ever round me move
Glorifying all things; for a little word,
Scarce ever meant at all, must I now prove

'Stone-cold for ever? Pray you, does the Lord
Will that all folks should be quite happy and good?
I love God now a little, if this cord

'Were broken, once for all what striving could
Make me love anything in earth or heaven.
So day by day it grew, as if one should

'Slip slowly down some path worn smooth and even,
Down to a cool sea on a summer day;
Yet still in slipping was there some small leaven

'Of stretched hands catching small stones by the way,
Until one surely reached the sea at last,
And felt strange new joy as the worn head lay

'Back, with the hair like sea-weed; yea all past
Sweat of the forehead, dryness of the lips,
Washed utterly out by the dear waves o'ercast

'In the lone sea, far off from any ships!
Do I not know now of a day in Spring?
No minute of that wild day ever slips

'From out my memory; I hear thrushes sing,
And wheresoever I may be, straightway
Thoughts of it all come up with most fresh sting;

'I was half mad with beauty on that day,
And went without my ladies all alone,
In a quiet garden walled round every way;

'I was right joyful of that wall of stone,
That shut the flowers and trees up with the sky,
And trebled all the beauty: to the bone,

'Yea right through to my heart, grown very shy
With weary thoughts, it pierced, and made me glad;
Exceedingly glad, and I knew verily,

24

'A little thing just then had made me mad;
I dared not think, as I was wont to do,
Sometimes, upon my beauty; if I had

'Held out my long hand up against the blue,
And, looking on the tenderly darken'd fingers,
Thought that by rights one ought to see quite through,

'There, see you, where the soft still light yet lingers,
Round by the edges; what should I have done,
If this had joined with yellow spotted singers,

'And startling green drawn upward by the sun?
But shouting, loosed out, see now! all my hair,
And trancedly stood watching the west wind run

'With faintest half-heard breathing sound — why there
I lose my head e'en now in doing this;
But shortly listen — In that garden fair

'Came Launcelot walking; this is true, the kiss
Wherewith we kissed in meeting that spring day,
I scarce dare talk of the remember'd bliss,

'When both our mouths went wandering in one way.
And aching sorely, met among the leaves;
Our hands being left behind strained far away.

'Never within a yard of my bright sleeves
Had Launcelot come before — and now, so nigh!
After that day why is it Guenevere grieves?

'Nevertheless you, O Sir Gauwaine, lie,
Whatever happened on through all those years,
God knows I speak truth, saying that you lie.

'Being such a lady could I weep these tears
If this were true? A great queen such as I
Having sinn'd this way, straight her conscience sears;

'And afterwards she liveth hatefully,
Slaying and poisoning, certes never weeps,—
Gauwaine be friends now, speak me lovingly.

'Do I not see how God's dear pity creeps
All through your frame, and trembles in your mouth?
Remember in what grave your mother sleeps,

'Buried in some place far down in the south,
Men are forgetting as I speak to you;
By her head sever'd in that awful drouth

'Of pity that drew Agravaine's fell blow,
I pray your pity! let me not scream out
For ever after, when the shrill winds blow

'Through half your castle-locks! let me not shout
For ever after in the winter night
When you ride out alone! in battle-rout

'Let not my rusting tears make your sword light!
Ah! God of mercy how he turns away!
So, ever must I dress me to the fight,

'So — let God's justice work! Gauwaine, I say,
See me hew down your proofs: yea all men know
Even as you said how Mellyagraunce one day,

'One bitter day in *la Fausse Garde*, for so
All good knights held it after, saw —
Yea, sirs, by cursed unknightly outrage; though

'You, Gauwaine, held his word without a flaw,
This Mellyagraunce saw blood upon my bed —
Whose blood then pray you? is there any law

'To make a queen say why some spots of red
Lie on her coverlet? or will you say,
"Your hands are white, lady, as when you wed,

' "Where did you bleed?" and must I stammer out — "Nay,
I blush indeed, fair lord, only to rend
My sleeve up to my shoulder, where there lay

' "A knife-point last night :" so must I defend
The honour of the Lady Guenevere?
Not so, fair lords, even if the world should end

'This very day, and you were judges here
Instead of God. Did you see Mellyagraunce
When Launcelot stood by him? what white fear

'Curdled his blood, and how his teeth did dance,
His side sink in? as my knight cried and said,
"Slayer of unarm'd men, here is a chance !

' "Setter of traps, I pray you guard your head,
By God I am so glad to fight with you,
Stripper of ladies, that my hand feels lead

' "For driving weight ; hurrah now ! draw and do,
For all my wounds are moving in my breast,
And I am getting mad with waiting so."

'He struck his hands together o'er the beast,
Who fell down flat, and grovell'd at his feet,
And groan'd at being slain so young — "at lcast."

'My knight said, "Rise you, sir, who are so fleet
At catching ladies, half-arm'd will I fight,
My left side all uncovered !" then I weet.

'Up sprang Sir Mellyagraunce with great delight
Upon his knave's face ; not until just then
Did I quite hate him, as I saw my knight

'Along the lists look to my stake and pen
With such a joyous smile, it made me sigh
From agony beneath my waist-chain, when

'The fight began, and to me they drew nigh;
Ever Sir Launcelot kept him on the right,
And traversed warily, and ever high

'And fast leapt caitiff's sword, until my knight
Sudden threw up his sword to his left hand,
Caught it, and swung it; that was all the fight.

'Except a spout of blood on the hot land;
For it was hottest summer; and I know
I wonder'd how the fire, while I should stand,

'And burn, against the heat, would quiver so,
Yards above my head; thus these matters went;
Which things were only warnings of the woe

'That fell on me. Yet Mellyagraunce was shent,
For Mellyagraunce had fought against the Lord;
Therefore, my lords, take heed lest you be blent

'With all this wickedness; say no rash word
Against me, being so beautiful; my eyes,
Wept all away to grey, may bring some sword

'To drown you in your blood; see my breast rise,
Like waves of purple sea, as here I stand;
And how my arms are moved in wonderful wise,

'Yea also at my full heart's strong command,
See through my long throat how the words go up
In ripples to my mouth; how in my hand

'The shadow lies like wine within a cup
Of marvellously colour'd gold; yea now
This little wind is rising, look you up,

'And wonder how the light is falling so
Within my moving tresses: will you dare,
When you have looked a little on my brow,

'To say this thing is vile? or will you care
For any plausible lies of cunning woof,
When you can see my face with no lie there

'For ever? am I not a gracious proof —
"But in your chamber Launcelot was found" —
Is there a good knight then would stand aloof,

'When a queen says with gentle queenly sound:
"O true as steel come now and talk with me,
I love to see your step upon the ground

' "Unwavering, also well I love to see
That gracious smile light up your face, and hear
Your wonderful words, that all mean verily

' "The thing they seem to mean: good friend, so dear
To me in everything, come here to-night,
Or else the hours will pass most dull and drear;

' "If you come not, I fear this time I might
Get thinking over much of times gone by,
When I was young, and green hope was in sight;

' "For no man cares now to know why I sigh;
And no man comes to sing me pleasant songs,
Nor any brings me the sweet flowers that lie

' "So thick in the gardens; therefore one so longs
To see you, Launcelot; that we may be
Like children once again, free from all wrongs

' "Just for one night." Did he not come to me?
What thing could keep true Launcelot away
If I said "come"? there was one less than three

'In my quiet room that night, and we were gay;
Till sudden I rose up, weak, pale, and sick,
Because a bawling broke our dream up, yea

'I looked at Launcelot's face and could not speak,
For he looked helpless too, for a little while;
Then I remember how I tried to shriek,

'And could not, but fell down; from tile to tile
The stones they threw up rattled o'er my head,
And made me dizzier; till within a while

'My maids were all about me, and my head
On Launcelot's breast was being soothed away
From its white chattering, until Launcelot said —

'By God! I will not tell you more to-day,
Judge any way you will — what matters it?
You know quite well the story of that fray,

'How Launcelot still'd their bawling, the mad fit
That caught up Gauwaine — all, all, verily,
But just that which would save me; these things flit.

'Nevertheless you, O Sir Gauwaine, lie,
Whatever may have happen'd these long years,
God knows I speak truth, saying that you lie!

'All I have said is truth, by Christ's dear tears.'
She would not speak another word, but stood
Turn'd sideways; listening, like a man who hears

His brother's trumpet sounding through the wood
Of his foes' lances. She lean'd eagerly,
And gave a slight spring sometimes, as she could

At last hear something really; joyfully
Her cheek grew crimson, as the headlong speed
Of the roan charger drew all men to see,
The knight who came was Launcelot at good need.

Sir Peter Harpdon's End

In an English Castle in Poictou

Sir Peter Harpdon, *a Gascon knight in the English service, and* John
Curzon, *his lieutenant*

JOHN CURZON

Of those three prisoners, that before you came
We took down at St. John's hard by the mill,
Two are good masons; we have tools enough,
And you have skill to set them working.

SIR PETER

         So —.

What are their names?

JOHN CURZON

     Why, Jacques Aquadent,
And Peter Plombiere, but —

SIR PETER

        What colour'd hair
Has Peter now? has Jacques got bow legs?

JOHN CURZON

Why, sir, you jest — what matters Jacques' hair,
Or Peter's legs to us?

SIR PETER

     O! John, John, John!
Throw all your mason's tools down the deep well,
Hang Peter up and Jacques; they're no good,
We shall not build, man.

JOHN CURZON (*going*)

     Shall I call the guard

To hang them, sir? and yet, sir, for the tools,
We'd better keep them still; sir, fare you well.

[Muttering as he goes

What have I done that he should jape at me?
And why not build? the walls are weak enough,
And we've two masons and a heap of tools.

[Goes, still muttering

SIR PETER

To think a man should have a lump like that
For his lieutenant! I must call him back,
Or else, as surely as St. George is dead,
He'll hang our friends the masons — here, John! John

JOHN CURZON

At your good service, sir.

SIR PETER

           Come now, and talk
This weighty matter out; there — we've no stone
To mend our walls with, — neither brick nor stone.

JOHN CURZON

There is a quarry, sir, some ten miles off.

SIR PETER

We are not strong enough to send ten men
Ten miles to fetch us stone enough to build,
In three hours' time they would be taken or slain,
The cursed Frenchmen ride abroad so thick.

JOHN CURZON

But we can send some villaynes to get stone.

SIR PETER

Alas! John, that we cannot bring them back,
They would go off to Clisson or Sanxere,

And tell them we were weak in walls and men,
Then down go we; for, look you, times are changed,
And now no longer does the country shake
At sound of English names; our captains fade
From off our muster-rolls. At Lusac bridge
I dare say you may even yet see the hole
That Chandos beat in dying; far in Spain
Pembroke is prisoner; Phelton prisoner here;
Manny lies buried in the Charterhouse;
Oliver Clisson turn'd these years agone;
The Captal died in prison; and, over all,
Edward the prince lies underneath the ground,
Edward the king is dead, at Westminster
The carvers smooth the curls of his long beard.
Everything goes to rack — eh! and we too.
Now, Curzon, listen; if they come, these French,
Whom have I got to lean on here, but you?
A man can die but once, will you die then,
Your brave sword in your hand, thoughts in your heart
Of all the deeds we have done here in France —
And yet may do? So God will have your soul,
Whoever has your body.

JOHN CURZON
Why, sir, I
Will fight till the last moment, until then
Will do whate'er you tell me. Now I see
We must e'en leave the walls; well, well, perhaps
They're stronger than I think for; pity, though!
For some few tons of stone, if Guesclin comes.

SIR PETER
Farewell, John, pray you watch the Gascons well,
I doubt them.

JOHN CURZON
Truly, sir, I will watch well.   [Goes

Farewell, good lump! and yet, when all is said,
'Tis a good lump. Why then, if Guesclin comes;
Some dozen stones from his petrariae,
And, under shelter of his crossbows, just
An hour's steady work with pickaxes,
Then a great noise — some dozen swords and glaives
A-playing on my basnet all at once,
And little more cross purposes on earth
For me.
      Now this is hard: a month ago,
And a few minutes' talk had set things right
'Twixt me and Alice; — if she had a doubt,
As (may Heaven bless her!) I scarce think she had,
'Twas but their hammer, hammer in her ears,
Of 'how Sir Peter fail'd at Lusac bridge:'
And 'how he was grown moody of late days;'
And 'how Sir Lambert' (think now!) 'his dear friend,
His sweet, dear cousin, could not but confess
That Peter's talk tended towards the French,
Which he' (for instance Lambert) 'was glad of,
Being' (Lambert, you see) 'on the French side.'
                        Well,
If I could but have seen her on that day,
Then, when they sent me off!
                  I like to think,
Although it hurts me, makes my head twist, what,
If I had seen her, what I should have said,
What she, my darling, would have said and done.
As thus perchance —
              To find her sitting there,
In the window-seat, not looking well at all,
Crying perhaps, and I say quietly;
'Alice!' she looks up, chokes a sob, looks grave,
Changes from pale to red, but, ere she speaks,
Straightway I kneel down there on both my knees
And say: 'O lady, have I sinn'd, your knight?
That still you ever let me walk alone

In the rose garden, that you sing no songs
When I am by, that ever in the dance
You quietly walk away when I come near?
Now that I have you, will you go, think you?'

   Ere she could answer I would speak again,
Still kneeling there.
                              'What! they have frighted you,
By hanging burs, and clumsily carven puppets,
Round my good name; but afterwards, my love,
I will say what this means; this moment, see!
Do I kneel here, and can you doubt me? Yea,'
(For she would put her hands upon my face,)
'Yea, that is best, yea feel, love, am I changed?'
And she would say: 'Good knight, come, kiss my lips!'
And afterwards as I sat there would say:

'Please a poor silly girl by telling me
What all those things they talk of really were,
For it is true you did not help Chandos,
And true, poor love! you could not come to me
When I was in such peril.'
                              I should say:
'I am like Balen, all things turn to blame —
I did not come to you? At Bergerath
The constable had held us close shut up,
If from the barriers I had made three steps,
I should have been but slain; at Lusac, too,
We struggled in a marish half the day,
And came too late at last: you know, my love,
How heavy men and horses are all arm'd.
All that Sir Lambert said was pure, unmix'd,
Quite groundless lies; as you can think, sweet love.'

She, holding tight my hand as we sat there,
Started a little at Sir Lambert's name,
But otherwise she listen'd scarce at all
To what I said. Then with moist, weeping eyes,

35

And quivering lips, that scarcely let her speak,
She said, 'I love you.'
                                    Other words were few,
The remnant of that hour; her hand smooth'd down
My foolish head; she kiss'd me all about
My face, and through the tangles of my beard
Her little fingers crept.
                              O! God, my Alice,
Not this good way: my lord but sent and said
That Lambert's sayings were taken at their worth,
Therefore that day I was to start, and keep
This hold against the French; and I am here, —
                              [*Looks out of the window*
A sprawling lonely gard with rotten walls,
And no one to bring aid if Guesclin comes,
Or any other.
                    There's a pennon now!
At last.
          But not the constable's, whose arms,
I wonder, does it bear? Three golden rings
On a red ground; my cousin's by the rood!
Well, I should like to kill him, certainly,
But to be kill'd by him —
                                    [*A trumpet sounds*
                    That's for a herald;
I doubt this does not mean assaulting yet.

                    Enter JOHN CURZON
What says the herald of our cousin, sir?

                    JOHN CURZON
So please you, sir, concerning your estate,
He has good will to talk with you.

                    SIR PETER
                              Outside,
I'll talk with him, close by the gate St. Ives.
Is he unarm'd?

Yea, sir, in a long gown.

SIR PETER

Then bid them bring me hither my furr'd gown
With the long sleeves, and under it I'll wear,
By Lambert's leave, a secret coat of mail;
And will you lend me, John, your little axe?
I mean the one with Paul wrought on the blade?
And I will carry it inside my sleeve,
Good to be ready always — you, John, go
And bid them set up many suits of arms,
Bows, archgays, lances, in the base-court, and
Yourself, from the south postern setting out,
With twenty men, be ready to break through
Their unguarded rear when I cry out 'St. George!'

JOHN CURZON

How, sir! will you attack him unawares,
And slay him unarm'd?

SIR PETER

Trust me, John, I know
The reason why he comes here with sleeved gown,
Fit to hide axes up. So, let us go.

[*They go*

*Outside the castle by the great gate; Sir Lambert and Sir Peter
seated; guards attending each, the rest of Sir Lambert's
men drawn up about a furlong off*

SIR PETER

And if I choose to take the losing side
Still, does it hurt you?

37

O ! no hurt to me;
I see you sneering, 'Why take trouble then,
Seeing you love me not?' look you, our house
(Which, taken altogether, I love much)
Had better be upon the right side now,
If, once for all, it wishes to bear rule
As such a house should : cousin, you're too wise
To feed your hope up fat, that this fair France
Will ever draw two ways again ; this side
The French, wrong-headed, all a-jar
With envious longings ; and the other side
The order'd English, orderly led on
By those two Edwards through all wrong and right,
And muddling right and wrong to a thick broth
With that long stick, their strength. This is all changed,
The true French win, on either side you have
Cool-headed men, good at a tilting match,
And good at setting battles in array,
And good at squeezing taxes at due time;
Therefore by nature we French being here
Upon our own big land —

[Sir Peter *laughs aloud*
Well, Peter ! well !
What makes you laugh?

SIR PETER

Hearing you sweat to prove
All this I know so well ; but you have read
The siege of Troy?

SIR LAMBERT
O ! yea, I know it well.

SIR PETER
There ! they were wrong, as wrong as men could be ;
For, as I think, they found it such delight

38

To see fair Helen going through their town:
Yea, any little common thing she did
(As stooping to pick a flower) seem'd so strange,
So new in its great beauty, that they said;
'Here we will keep her living in this town,
Till all burns up together.' And so, fought,
In a mad whirl of knowing they were wrong;
Yea, they fought well, and ever, like a man
That hangs legs off the ground by both his hands,
Over some great height, did they struggle sore,
Quite sure to slip at last; wherefore, take note
How almost all men, reading that sad siege,
Hold for the Trojans; as I did at least,
Thought Hector the best knight a long way:

                                             Now

Why should I not do this thing that I think,
For even when I come to count the gains,
I have them my side: men will talk, you know,
(We talk of Hector, dead so long agone,)
When I am dead, of how this Peter clung
To what he thought the right; of how he died,
Perchance, at last, doing some desperate deed
Few men would care do now, and this is gain
To me, as ease and money is to you,
Moreover, too, I like the straining game
Of striving well to hold up things that fall;
So one becomes great; see you! in good times
All men live well together, and you, too,
Live dull and happy — happy? not so quick,
Suppose sharp thoughts begin to burn you up.
Why then, but just to fight as I do now,
A halter round my neck, would be great bliss.
O! I am well off.   *[Aside*
                  Talk, and talk, and talk,
I know this man has come to murder me,
And yet I talk still.

SIR LAMBERT

If your side were right,
You might be, though you lost; but if I said,
'You are a traitor, being, as you are,
Born Frenchman.' What are Edwards unto you,
Or Richards?

SIR PETER

Nay, hold there, my Lambert, hold!
For fear your zeal should bring you to some harm,
Don't call me traitor

SIR LAMBERT

Furthermore, my knight,
Men call you slippery on your losing side,
When at Bordeaux I was ambassador,
I heard them say so, and could scarce say 'Nay.'
                    [*He takes hold of something in his sleeve, and rises*

SIR PETER (*rising*)

They lied — and you lie, not for the first time.
What have you got there, fumbling up your sleeve,
A stolen purse?

SIR LAMBERT

Nay, liar in your teeth!
Dead liar too; St. Dennis and St. Lambert!
                    [*Strikes at* Sir Peter *with a dagger*

SIR PETER (*striking him flatlings with his axe*)

How thief! thief! thief! so there, fair thief, so there,
St. George Guienne! glaives for the castellan!
You French, you are but dead, unless you lay
Your spears upon the earth. St. George Guienne!

Well done, John Curzon, how he has them now.

40

JOHN CURZON

What shall we do with all these prisoners, sir?

SIR PETER

Why put them all to ransom, those that can
Pay anything, but not too light though, John,
Seeing we have them on the hip : for those
That have no money, that being certified,
Why turn them out of doors before they spy ;
But bring Sir Lambert guarded unto me.

JOHN CURZON

I will, fair sir.   [*He goes*

SIR PETER

            I do not wish to kill him,
Although I think I ought ; he shall go mark'd,
By all the saints, though !

            Enter Lambert (*guarded*)
                        Now, Sir Lambert, now !
What sort of death do you expect to get,
Being taken this way?

SIR LAMBERT

                        Cousin ! cousin ! think !
I am your own blood ; may God pardon me !
I am not fit to die ; if you knew all,
All I have done since I was young and good.
O ! you would give me yet another chance,
As God would, that I might wash all clear out,
By serving you and Him. Let me go now !
And I will pay you down more golden crowns
Of ransom than the king would !

41

SIR PETER

> Well, stand back,
And do not touch me! No, you shall not die,
Nor yet pay ransom. You, John Curzon, cause
Some carpenters to build a scaffold, high,
Outside the gate; when it is built, sound out
To all good folks, 'Come, see a traitor punish'd!'
Take me my knight, and set him up thereon,
And let the hangman shave his head quite clean,
And cut his ears off close up to the head;
And cause the minstrels all the while to play
Soft music, and good singing, for this day
Is my high day of triumph; is it not,
Sir Lambert?

SIR LAMBERT

> Ah! on your own blood,
Own name, you heap this foul disgrace? you dare,
With hands and fame thus sullied, to go back
And take the Lady Alice —

SIR PETER

> Say her name
Again, and you are dead, slain here by me.
Why should I talk with you, I'm master here,
And do not want your schooling; is it not
My mercy that you are not dangling dead
There in the gateway with a broken neck?

SIR LAMBERT

Such mercy! why not kill me then outright?
To die is nothing; but to live that all
May point their fingers! yea, I'd rather die.

JOHN CURZON

Why, will it make you any uglier man
To lose your ears? they're much too big for you.
You ugly Judas!

Hold, John!   [*To* Lambert
                    That's your choice,
To die, mind! Then you shall die — Lambert mine,
I thank you now for choosing this so well,
It saves me much perplexity and doubt;
Perchance an ill deed too, for half I count
This sparing traitors is an ill deed.
                              Well,
Lambert, die bravely, and we're almost friends.

SIR LAMBERT, *grovelling*

O God! this is a fiend and not a man;
Will some one save me from him? help, help, help!
I will not die.

SIR PETER

Why, what is this I see?
A man who is a knight, and bandied words
So well just now with me, is lying down,
Gone mad for fear like this! So, so, you thought
You knew the worst, and might say what you pleased.
I should have guess'd this from a man like you.
Eh! righteous Job would give up skin for skin,
Yea, all a man can have for simple life,
And we talk fine, yea, even a hound like this,
Who needs must know that when he dies, deep hell
Will hold him fast for ever — so fine we talk,
'Would rather die' — all that. Now sir, get up!
And choose again: shall it be head sans ears,
Or trunk sans head?
                    John Curzon, pull him up!
What, life then? go and build the scaffold, John.

Lambert, I hope that never on this earth
We meet again; that you'll turn out a monk,
And mend the life I give you, so farewell,
I'm sorry you're a rascal. John, despatch.

Sir Peter *prisoner*, Guesclin, Clisson, Sir Lambert

SIR PETER

So now is come the ending of my life;
If I could clear this sickening lump away
That sticks in my dry throat, and say a word,
Guesclin might listen.

GUESCLIN

            Tell me, fair sir knight,
If you have been clean liver before God,
And then you need not fear much; as for me,
I cannot say I hate you, yet my oath,
And cousin Lambert's ears here clench the thing.

SIR PETER

I knew you could not hate me, therefore I
Am bold to pray for life;'twill harm your cause
To hang knights of good name, harm here in France
I have small doubt, at any rate hereafter
Men will remember you another way
Than I should care to be remember'd, ah!
Although hot lead runs through me for my blood,
All this falls cold as though I said, 'Sweet lords,
Give back my falcon!'
           See how young I am,
Do you care altogether more than France,
Say rather one French faction, than for all
The state of Christendom? a gallant knight,
As (yea, by God!) I have been, is more worth
Than many castles; will you bring this death,
For a mere act of justice, on my head?

Think how it ends all, death! all other things
Can somehow be retrieved, yea, send me forth
Naked and maimed, rather than slay me here;
Then somehow will I get me other clothes,

44

And somehow will I get me some poor horse,
And, somehow clad in poor old rusty arms,
Will ride and smite among the serried glaives,
Fear not death so; for I can tilt right well,
Let me not say 'I could;' I know all tricks,
That sway the sharp sword cunningly; ah you,
You, my Lord Clisson, in the other days
Have seen me learning these, yea, call to mind,
How in the trodden corn by Chartrés town,
When you were nearly swooning from the back
Of your black horse, those three blades slid at once
From off my sword's edge; pray for me, my lord!

CLISSON

Nay, this is pitiful, to see him die.
My Lord the Constable, I pray you note
That you are losing some few thousand crowns
By slaying this man; also think; his lands
Along the Garonne river lie for leagues,
And are right rich, a many mills he has,
Three abbeys of grey monks do hold of him,
Though wishing well for Clement, as we do;
I know the next heir, his old uncle, well,
Who does not care two deniers for the knight
As things go now, but slay him, and then see,
How he will bristle up like any perch,
With curves of spears. What! do not doubt, my lord,
You'll get the money, this man saved my life,
And I will buy him for two thousand crowns;
Well, five then — eh! what! 'No' again? well then,
Ten thousand crowns?

GUESCLIN

                    My sweet lord, much I grieve
I cannot please you, yea, good sooth, I grieve
This knight must die, as verily he must;
For I have sworn it, so men take him out,
Use him not roughly.

45

Music, do you know,
Music will suit you well, I think, because
You look so mild, like Laurence being grill'd;
Or perhaps music soft and low, because
This is high day of triumph unto me,
Is it not, Peter?

You are frighten'd, though,
Eh! you are pale, because this hurts you much,
Whose life was pleasant to you, not like mine,
You ruin'd wretch! Men mock me in the streets,
Only in whispers loud, because I am
Friend of the constable; will this please you,
Unhappy Peter? once a-going home,
Without my servants, and a little drunk,
At midnight through the lone dim lamp-lit streets,
A whore came up and spat into my eyes,
(Rather to blind me than to make me see,)
But she was very drunk, and tottering back,
Even in the middle of her laughter, fell
And cut her head against the pointed stones,
While I lean'd on my staff, and look'd at her,
And cried, being drunk.

Girls would not spit at you,
You are so handsome, I think verily
Most ladies would be glad to kiss your eyes,
And yet you will be hung like a cur dog
Five minutes hence, and grow black in the face,
And curl your toes up. Therefore I am glad.

Guess why I stand and talk this nonsense now,
With Guesclin getting ready to play chess,
And Clisson doing something with his sword,
I can't see what, talking to Guesclin though,
I don't know what about, perhaps of you,
But, cousin Peter, while I stroke your beard,
Let me say this, I'd like to tell you now
That your life hung upon a game of chess,

46

That if, say, my squire Robert here should beat,
Why you should live, but hang if I beat him;
Then guess, clever Peter, what I should do then;
Well, give it up? why, Peter, I should let
My squire Robert beat me, then you would think
That you were safe, you know: Eh? not at all,
But I should keep you three days in some hold,
Giving you salt to eat, which would be kind,
Considering the tax there is on salt;
And afterwards should let you go, perhaps?
No I should not, but I should hang you, sir,
With a red rope in lieu of mere grey rope.

But I forgot, you have not told me yet
If you can guess why I talk nonsense thus,
Instead of drinking wine while you are hang'd?
You are not quick at guessing, give it up.
This is the reason; here I hold your hand,
And watch you growing paler, see you writhe,
And this, my Peter, is a joy so dear,
I cannot by all striving tell you how
I love it, nor I think, good man, would you
Quite understand my great delight therein;
You, when you had me underneath you once,
Spat as it were, and said, 'Go take him out,'
(That they might do that thing to me whereat,
E'en now this long time off I could well shriek,)
And then you tried forget I ever lived,
And sunk your hating into other things;
While I — St. Dennis! though, I think you'll faint,
Your lips are grey so; yes, you will, unless
You let it out and weep like a hurt child;
Hurrah! you do now. Do not go just yet,
For I am Alice, am right like her now;
Will you not kiss me on the lips, my love? —

You filthy beast, stand back and let him go,
Or by God's eyes I'll choke you.

[*Kneeling to* Sir Peter
                                Fair sir knight,
I kneel upon my knees and pray to you
That you would pardon me for this your death;
God knows how much I wish you still alive,
Also how heartily I strove to save
Your life at this time; yea, he knows quite well,
(I swear it, so forgive me!) how I would,
If it were possible, give up my life
Upon this grass for yours; fair knight, although,
He knowing all things knows this thing too, well,
Yet when you see his face some short time hence,
Tell him I tried to save you.

                    SIR PETER
                                O! my lord,
I cannot say this is as good as life,
But yet it makes me feel far happier now,
And if at all, after a thousand years,
I see God's face, I will speak loud and bold,
And tell Him you were kind, and like Himself;
Sir! may God bless you!
                                Did you note how I
Fell weeping just now? pray you, do not think
That Lambert's taunts did this, I hardly heard
The base things that he said, being deep in thought
Of all things that have happen'd since I was
A little child; and so at last I thought
Of my true lady: truly, sir, it seem'd
No longer gone than yesterday, that this
Was the sole reason God let me be born
Twenty-five years ago, that I might love
Her, my sweet lady, and be loved by her;
This seem'd so yesterday, to-day death comes,

And is so bitter strong, I cannot see
Why I was born.
              But as a last request,
I pray you, O kind Clisson, send some man,
Some good man, mind you, to say how I died,
And take my last love to her; fare-you-well,
And may God keep you; I must go now, lest
I grow too sick with thinking on these things;
Likewise my feet are wearied of the earth,
From whence I shall be lifted upright soon.

                                     [As he goes

Ah me! shamed too, I wept at fear of death;
And yet not so, I only wept because
There was no beautiful lady to kiss me
Before I died, and sweetly wish good speed
From her dear lips. O for some lady, though
I saw here ne'er before; Alice, my love,
I do not ask for; Clisson was right kind,
If he had been a woman, I should die
Without this sickness: but I am all wrong,
So wrong and hopelessly afraid to die.
There, I will go.
              My God! how sick I am,
If only she could come and kiss me now.

The Hotel de la Barde, Bordeaux

The Lady Alice de la Barde *looking out of a window
into the street*

No news yet! surely, still he holds his own;
That garde stands well; I mind me passing it
Some months ago; God grant the walls are strong!
I heard some knights say something yestereve,
I tried hard to forget: words far apart
Struck on my heart; something like this; one said
'What eh! a Gascon with an English name,
Harpdon?' then nought, but afterwards, 'Poictou.'
As one who answers to a question ask'd;

Then carelessly regretful came, 'No, no.'
Whereto in answer loud and eagerly,
One said, 'Impossible? Christ, what foul play!'
And went off angrily; and while thenceforth
I hurried gaspingly afraid, I heard,
'Guesclin;' 'Five thousand men-at-arms;' 'Clisson.'
My heart misgives me it is all in vain
I send these succours; and in good time there!
Their trumpet sounds, ah! here they are; good knights,
God up in Heaven keep you.

                     If they come
And find him prisoner — for I can't believe
Guesclin will slay him, even though they storm —
(The last horse turns the corner.)

                             God in Heaven!
What have I got to thinking of at last!
That thief I will not name is with Guesclin,
Who loves him for his lands. My love! my love!
O, if I lose you after all the past,
What shall I do?

                  I cannot bear the noise
And light street out there, with this thought alive,
Like any curling snake within my brain;
Let me just hide my head within these soft
Deep cushions, there to try and think it out.
                             [*Lying in the window-seat*
I cannot hear much noise now, and I think
That I shall go to sleep: it all sounds dim
And faint, and I shall soon forget most things;
Yea, almost that I am alive and here;
It goes slow, comes slow, like a big mill-wheel
On some broad stream, with long green weeds a-sway,
And soft and slow it rises and it falls,
Still going onward.

                  Lying so, one kiss,
And I should be in Avalon asleep,
Among the poppies, and the yellow flowers;
And they should brush my cheek, my hair being spread

Far out among the stems; soft mice and small
Eating and creeping all about my feet,
Red shod and tired; and the flies should come
Creeping o'er my broad eyelids unafraid;
And there should be a noise of water going,
Clear blue, fresh water breaking on the slates,
Likewise the flies should creep — God's eyes! God help,
A trumpet? I will run fast, leap adown
The slippery sea-stairs, where the crabs fight.
                                        Ah!
I was half dreaming, but the trumpet's true,
He stops here at our house. The Clisson arms?
Ah, now for news. But I must hold my heart,
And be quite gentle till he is gone out:
And afterwards, — but he is still alive,
He must be still alive.

                Enter a Squire *of* Clisson's

                Good day, fair sir,
I give you welcome, knowing whence you come.

                SQUIRE
My Lady Alice de la Barde, I come
From Oliver Clisson, knight and mighty lord,
Bringing you tidings: I make bold to hope
You will not count me villain, even if
They wring your heart; nor hold me still in hate.
For I am but a mouthpiece after all,
A mouthpiece, too, of one who wishes well
To you and your's.

                ALICE
                Can you talk faster, sir,
Get over all this quicker? fix your eyes
On mine, I pray you, and whate'er you see,
Still go on talking fast, unless I fall,
Or bid you stop.

                51

I pray your pardon then,
And, looking in your eyes, fair lady, say
I am unhappy that your knight is dead.
Take heart, and listen! let me tell you all.
We were five thousand goodly men-at-arms,
And scant five hundred had he in that hold;
His rotten sand-stone walls were wet with rain,
And fell in lumps wherever a stone hit;
Yet for three days about the barrier there
The deadly glaives were gathered, laid across,
And push'd and pull'd; the fourth our engines came;
But still amid the crash of falling walls,
And roar of lombards, rattle of hard bolts,
The steady bow-strings flash'd, and still stream'd out
St. George's banner, and seven swords,
And still they cried, 'St. George Guienne,' until
Their walls were flat as Jericho's of old,
And our rush came, and cut them from the keep.

ALICE

Stop sir, and tell me if you slew him then,
And where he died, if you can really mean
That Peter Harpdon, the good knight, is dead?

SQUIRE

Fair lady, in the base-court —

ALICE

                              What base-court?
What do you talk of? Nay, go on, go on;
'Twas only something gone within my head:
Do you not know, one turns one's head round quick,
And something cracks there with sore pain? go on,
And still look at my eyes.

SQUIRE
                    Almost alone,

There in the base-court fought he with his sword,
Using his left hand much, more than the wont
Of most knights now-a-days; our men gave back,
For wheresoever he hit a downright blow,
Some one fell bleeding, for no plate could hold
Against the sway of body and great arm;
Till he grew tired, and some man (no! not I,
I swear not I, fair lady, as I live!)
Thrust at him with a glaive between the knees,
And threw him; down he fell, sword undermost;
Many fell on him, crying out their cries,
Tore his sword from him, tore his helm off, and —

ALICE

Yea, slew him; I am much too young to live,
Fair God, so let me die.
                    You have done well,
Done all your message gently, pray you go,
Our knights will make you cheer; moreoever, take
This bag of franks for your expenses.

                                [*The* Squire *kneels*

                    But
You do not go; still looking at my face,
You kneel! what, squire, do you mock me then?
You need not tell me who has set you on,
But tell me only, 'tis a made-up tale.
You are some lover may-be, or his friend;
Sir, if you loved me once, or your friend loved,
Think, is it not enough that I kneel down
And kiss your feet, your jest will be right good
If you give in now, carry it too far,
And 'twill be cruel; not yet? but you weep
Almost, as though you loved me; love me then,
And go to Heaven by telling all your sport,
And I will kiss you, then with all my heart,
Upon the mouth; O! what can I do then
To move you?

Lady fair, forgive me still!
You know I am so sorry, but my tale
Is not yet finish'd:
So they bound his hands,
And brought him tall and pale to Guesclin's tent,
Who, seeing him, leant his head upon his hand,
And ponder'd somewhile, afterwards, looking up —
Fair dame, what shall I say?

ALICE

Yea, I know now,
Good squire, you may go now with my thanks.

SQUIRE

Yet, lady, for your own sake I say this,
Yea, for my own sake, too, and Clisson's sake.
When Guesclin told him he must be hanged soon,
Within a while he lifted up his head
And spoke for his own life; not crouching, though,
As abjectly afraid to die, nor yet
Sullenly brave as many a thief will die;
Nor yet as one that plays at japes with God:
Few words he spoke; not so much what he said
Moved us, I think, as, saying it, there played
Strange tenderness from that big soldier there
About his pleading; eagerness to live
Because folk loved him, and he loved them back,
And many gallant plans unfinish'd now
For ever. Clisson's heart, which may God bless!
Was moved to pray for him, but all in vain;
Wherefore I bring this message:
Then he waits,
Still loving you, within the little church
Whose windows, with the one eye of the light
Over the altar, every night behold
The great dim broken walls he strove to keep!

There my Lord Clisson did his burial well.
Now, lady, I will go; God give you rest!

ALICE

Thank Clisson from me, squire, and farewell!
And now to keep myself from going mad.
Christ! I have been a many times to church,
And, ever since my mother taught me prayers,
Have used them daily, but to-day I wish
To pray another way; come face to face,
O Christ, that I may clasp your knees and pray,
I know not what, at any rate come now
From one of many places where you are;
Either in Heaven amid thick angel wings,
Or sitting on the altar strange with gems,
Or high up in the dustiness of the apse;
Let us go, You and I, a long way off,
To the little damp, dark, Poitevin church;
While you sit on the coffin in the dark,
Will I lie down, my face on the bare stone
Between your feet, and chatter anything
I have heard long ago, what matters it
So I may keep you there, your solemn face
And long hair even-flowing on each side,
Until you love me well enough to speak,
And give me comfort; yea, till o'er your chin,
And cloven red beard the great tears roll down
In pity for my misery, and I die,
Kissed over by you.
                    Eh Guesclin! if I were
Like Countess Mountfort now, that kiss'd the knight,
Across the salt sea come to fight for her;
Ah! just to go about with many knights,
Wherever you went, and somehow on one day,
In a thick wood to catch you off your guard,
Let you find, you and your some fifty friends,
Nothing but arrows wheresoe'er you turn'd,
Yea, and red crosses, great spears over them;

55

And so, between a lane of my true men,
To walk up pale and stern and tall, and with
My arms on my surcoat, and his therewith,
And then to make you kneel, O knight, Guesclin;
And then — alas! alas! when all is said,
What could I do but let you go again,
Being pitiful woman? I get no revenge,
Whatever happens; and I get no comfort,
I am but weak, and cannot move my feet,
But as men bid me.
                              Strange I do not die.
Suppose this had not happen'd after all;
I will lean out again and watch for news.

I wonder how long I can still feel thus,
As though I watch'd for news, feel as I did
Just half-an-hour ago, before this news.
How all the street is humming, some men sing,
And some men talk; some look up at the house,
Then lay their heads together and look grave;
Their laughter pains me sorely in the heart,
Their thoughtful talking makes my head turn round,
Yea, some men sing, what is it then they sing?
Eh Launcelot, and love and fate and death;
They ought to sing of him who was as wight
As Launcelot or Wade, and yet avail'd
Just nothing, but to fail and fail and fail,
And so at last to die and leave me here,
Alone and wretched; yea, perhaps they will,
When many years are past, make songs of us;
God help me, though, truly I never thought
That I should make a story in this way,
A story that his eyes can never see.

[One sings from outside]

Therefore be it believed
Whatsoever he grieved,
Whan his horse was relieved,
  This Launcelot,

Beat down on his knee,
Right valiant was he
God's body to see,
  Though he saw it not.

Right valiant to move
But for his sad love
The high God above
  Stinted his praise.

Yet so he was glad
That his son Lord Galahad
That high joyaunce had
  All his life-days.

Sing we therefore then
Launcelot's praise again,
For he wan crownés ten,
  If he wan not twelve.

To his death from his birth
He was muckle of worth,
Lay him in the cold earth,
  A long grave ye may delve.

Omnes homines benedicite!
This last fitte ye may see,
All men pray for me,
Who made this history
Cunning and fairly.

Concerning Geffray Teste Noire

And if you meet the Canon of Chimay,
    As going to Ortaise you well may do,
Greet him from John of Castel Neuf, and say,
    All that I tell you, for all this is true.

This Geffray Teste Noire was a Gascon thief,
    Who, under shadow of the English name,
Pilled all such towns and countries as were lief
    To King Charles and St. Dennis; thought it blame

If anything escaped him; so my lord,
    The Duke of Berry, sent Sir John Bonne Lance,
And other knights, good players with the sword,
    To check this thief, and give the land a chance.

Therefore we set our bastides round the tower
    That Geffray held, the strong thief! like a king,
High perch'd upon the rock of Ventadour,
    Hopelessly strong by Christ! it was mid spring,

When first I joined the little army there
    With ten good spears; Auvergne is hot, each day
We sweated armed before the barrier,
    Good feats of arms were done there often — eh?

You brother was slain there? I mind me now
    A right, good man-at-arms, God pardon him!
I think 'twas Geffray smote him on the brow
    With some spiked axe, and while he totter'd, dim

About the eyes, the spear of Alleyne Roux
    Slipped through his camaille and his throat; well, well!
Alleyne is paid now; your name Alleyne too?
    Mary! how strange — but this tale I would tell —

For spite of all our bastides, damned blackhead
    Would ride abroad, whene'er he chose to ride,
We could not stop him ; many a burgher bled
    Dear gold all round his girdle ; far and wide

The villaynes dwelt in utter misery
    'Twixt us and thief Sir Geffray ; hauled this way
By Sir Bonne Lance at one time, he gone by,
    Down comes this Teste Noire on another day.

And therefore they dig up the stone, grind corn,
    Hew wood, draw water, yea, they lived, in short,
As I said just now, utterly forlorn,
    Till this our knave and blackhead was out-fought.

So Bonne Lance fretted, thinking of some trap
    Day after day, till on a time he said ;
'John of Newcastle, if we have good hap,
    We catch our thief in two days.' 'How?' I said.

'Why, Sir, to-day he rideth out again,
    Hoping to take well certain sumpter mules
From Carcassonne, going with little train,
    Because, forsooth, he thinketh us mere fools ;

'But if we set an ambush in some wood,
    He is but dead : so, Sir, take thirty spears
To Verville forest, if it seem you good.'
    Then felt I like the horse in Job, who hears

The dancing trumpet sound, and we went forth ;
    And my red lion on the spear-head flapped,
As faster than the cool wind we rode North,
    Towards the wood of Verville ; thus it happed.

We rode a soft space on that day while spies
    Got news about Sir Geffray, the red wine
Under the road-side bush was clear ; the flies,
    The dragon-flies I mind me most, did shine

In brighter arms than ever I put on;
　So — 'Geffray,' said our spies, 'would pass that way
Next day at sundown;' then he must be won;
　And so we enter'd Verville wood next day,

In the afternoon; through it the highway runs,
　'Twixt copses of green hazel, very thick,
And underneath, with glimmering of suns,
　The primroses are happy; the dews lick

The soft green moss. 'Put cloths about your arms,
　Lest they should glitter; surely they will go
In a long thin line, watchful for alarms,
　With all their carriages of booty, so —

'Lay down my pennon in the grass — Lord God!
　What have we lying here? will they be cold,
I wonder, being so bare, above the sod,
　Instead of under? This was a knight too, fold

'Lying on fold of ancient rusted mail;
　No plate at all, gold rowels to the spurs,
And see the quiet gleam of turquoise pale
　Along the ceinture; but the long time blurs

'Even the tinder of his coat to nought,
　Except these scraps of leather; see how white
The skull is, loose within the coif! He fought
　A good fight, maybe, ere he was slain quite.

'No armour on the legs too; strange in faith —
　A little skeleton for a knight though — ah!
This one is bigger, truly without scathe
　His enemies escaped not — ribs driven out far, —

'That must have reach'd the heart, I doubt — how now,
　What say you, Aldovrand — a woman? why?'
'Under the coif a gold wreath on the brow,
　Yea, see the hair not gone to powder, lie,

60

'Golden, no doubt, once — yea, and very small —
    This for a knight; but for a dame, my lord,
These loose-hung bones seem shapely still, and tall, —
    Didst ever see a woman's bones, my lord?'

Often, God help me! I remember when
    I was a simple boy, fifteen years old,
The Jacquerie froze up the blood of men
    With their fell deeds, not fit now to be told:

God help again! we enter'd Beauvais town,
    Slaying them fast, whereto I help'd, mere boy
As I was then; we gentles cut them down,
    These burners and defilers, with great joy.

Reason for that, too, in the great church there
    These fiends had lit a fire, that soon went out,
The church at Beauvais being so great and fair —
    My father, who was by me, gave a shout

Between a beast's howl and a woman's scream,
    Then, panting, chuckled to me: 'John, look! look!
Count the dames' skeletons!' From some bad dream
    Like a man just awaked, my father shook;

And I, being faint with smelling the burnt bones,
    And very hot with fighting down the street,
And sick of such a life, fell down, with groans
    My head went weakly nodding to my feet. —

— An arrow had gone through her tender throat,
    And her right wrist was broken; then I saw
The reason why she had on that war-coat,
    Their story came out clear without a flaw;

For when he knew that they were being waylaid,
    He threw it over her, yea, hood and all;
Whereby he was much hack'd, while they were stay'd
    By those their murderers; many an one did fall

Beneath his arm, no doubt, so that he clear'd
   Their circle, bore his death-wound out of it;
But as they rode, some archer least afear'd
   Drew a strong bow, and thereby she was hit.

Still as he rode he knew not she was dead,
   Thought her but fainted from her broken wrist,
He bound with his great leathern belt — she bled?
   Who knows! he bled too, neither was there miss'd

The beating of her heart, his heart beat well
   For both of them, till here, within this wood,
He died scarce sorry; easy this to tell;
   After these years the flowers forget their blood. —

I saw you kissing once, like a curved sword
   That bites with all its edge, did your lips lie,
Curled gently, slowly, long time could afford
   For caught-up breathings: like a dying sigh

They gather'd up their lines and went away,
   And still kept twitching with a sort of smile,
As likely to be weeping presently, —
   Your hands too — how I watch'd them all the while!

'Cry out St. Peter now,' quoth Aldovrand;
   I cried, 'St. Peter,' broke out from the wood
With all my spears; we met them hand to hand,
   And shortly slew them; natheless, by the rood,

We caught not blackhead then, or any day;
   Months after that he died at last in bed,
From a wound pick'd up at a barrier-fray;
   That same year's end a steel bolt in the head,

And much bad living kill'd Teste Noire at last;
   John Froissart knoweth he is dead by now,
No doubt, but knoweth not this tale just past;
   Perchance then you can tell him what I show.

In my new castle, down beside the Eure,
    There is a little chapel of squared stone,
Painted inside and out; in green nook pure
    There did I lay them, every wearied bone;

And over it they lay, with stone-white hands
    Clasped fast together, hair made bright with gold
This Jaques Picard, known through many lands,
    Wrought cunningly; he's dead now — I am old.

Shameful Death

There were four of us about that bed;
    The mass-priest knelt at the side,
I and his mother stood at the head,
    Over his feet lay the bride;
We were quite sure that he was dead,
    Though his eyes were open wide.

He did not die in the night,
    He did not die in the day,
But in the morning twilight
    His spirit pass'd away,
When neither sun nor moon was bright,
    And the trees were merely grey.

He was not slain with the sword,
    Knight's axe, or the knightly spear,
Yet spoke he never a word
    After he came in here;
I cut away the cord
    From the neck of my brother dear.

He did not strike one blow,
　　For the recreants came behind,
In a place where the hornbeams grow,
　　A path right hard to find,
For the hornbeam boughs swing so,
　　That the twilight makes it blind.

They lighted a great torch then,
　　When his arms were pinion'd fast,
Sir John the knight of the Fen,
　　Sir Guy of the Dolorous Blast,
With knights threescore and ten,
　　Hung brave Lord Hugh at last.

I am threescore and ten,
　　And my hair is all turn'd grey,
But I met Sir John of the Fen
　　Long ago on a summer day,
And am glad to think of the moment when
　　I took his life away.

I am threescore and ten,
　　And my strength is mostly pass'd,
But long ago I and my men
　　When the sky was overcast,
And the smoke roll'd over the reeds of the fen,
　　Slew Guy of the Dolorous Blast.

And now, knights all of you,
　　I pray you pray for Sir Hugh,
A good knight and a true,
　　And for Alice, his wife, pray too.

The Sailing of the Sword

Across the empty garden-beds,
  When the Sword went out to sea,
I scarcely saw my sisters' heads
  Bowed each beside a tree.
I could not see the castle leads,
  When the Sword went out to sea.

Alicia wore a scarlet gown,
  When the Sword went out to sea,
But Ursula's was russet brown:
  For the mist we could not see
The scarlet roofs of the good town,
  When the Sword went out to sea.

Green holly in Alicia's hand,
  When the Sword went out to sea;
With sere oak-leaves did Ursula stand;
  O! yet alas for me!
I did but bear a peel'd white wand,
  When the Sword went out to sea.

O, russet brown and scarlet bright,
  When the Sword went out to sea,
My sisters wore; I wore but white:
  Red, brown, and white, are three;
Three damozels; each had a knight,
  When the Sword went out to sea.

Sir Robert shouted loud, and said,
  When the Sword went out to sea,
'Alicia, while I see thy head,
  What shall I bring for thee?'
'O, my sweet lord, a ruby red:'
  The Sword went out to sea.

Sir Miles said, while the sails hung down,
  When the Sword went out to sea,

'Oh, Ursula! while I see the town,
    What shall I bring for thee?'
'Dear knight, bring back a falcon brown:'
    The Sword went out to sea.

But my Roland, no word he said
    When the Sword went out to sea;
But only turn'd away his head, —
    A quick shriek came from me:
'Come back, dear lord, to your white maid;' —
    The Sword went out to sea.

The hot sun bit the garden-beds,
    When the Sword came back from sea;
Beneath an apple-tree our heads
    Stretched out toward the sea;
Grey gleam'd the thirsty castle-leads,
    When the Sword came back from sea.

Lord Robert brought a ruby red,
    When the Sword came back from sea;
He kissed Alicia on the head:
    'I am come back to thee;
'Tis time, sweet love, that we were wed,
    Now the Sword is back from sea!'

Sir Miles he bore a falcon brown,
    When the Sword came back from sea;
His arms went round tall Ursula's gown, —
    'What joy, O love, but thee?
Let us be wed in the good town,
    Now the Sword is back from sea!'

My heart grew sick, no more afraid,
    When the Sword came back from sea;
Upon the deck a tall white maid
    Sat on Lord Roland's knee;
His chin was press'd upon her head,
    When the Sword came back from sea!

The Blue Closet

THE DAMOZELS

Lady Alice, Lady Louise,
Between the wash of the tumbling seas
We are ready to sing, if so ye please;
So lay your long hands on the keys;
   Sing, 'Laudate pueri.'

And ever the great bell overhead
Boom'd in the wind a knell for the dead,
Though no one toll'd it, a knell for the dead.

LADY LOUISE

Sister, let the measure swell
Not too loud; for you sing not well
If you drown the faint boom of the bell;
   He is weary, so am I.

And ever the chevron overhead
Flapp'd on the banner of the dead;
(Was he asleep, or was he dead?)

LADY ALICE

Alice the Queen, and Louise the Queen,
Two damozels wearing purple and green,
Four lone ladies dwelling here
From day to day and year to year;
And there is none to let us go;
To break the locks of the doors below,
Or shovel away the heaped-up snow;
And when we die no man will know
That we are dead; but they give us leave,
Once every year on Christmas-eve,
To sing in the Closet Blue one song;
And we should be so long, so long,
If we dared, in singing; for dream on dream,
They float on in a happy stream;

Float from the gold strings, float from the keys,
Float from the open'd lips of Louise;
But, alas! the sea-salt oozes through
The chinks of the tiles of the Closet Blue;
And ever the great bell overhead
Booms in the wind a knell for the dead,
The wind plays on it a knell for the dead.

[*They sing all together.*]

How long ago was it, how long ago,
He came to this tower with hands full of snow?

'Kneel down, O love Louise, kneel down,' he said,
And sprinkled the dusty snow over my head.

He watch'd the snow melting, it ran through my hair,
Ran over my shoulders, white shoulders and bare.

'I cannot weep for thee, poor love Louise,
For my tears are all hidden deep under the seas;

'In a gold and blue casket she keeps all my tears,
But my eyes are no longer blue, as in old years;

'Yea, they grow grey with time, grow small and dry,
I am so feeble now, would I might die.'

    And in truth the great bell overhead
    Left off his pealing for the dead,
    Perchance, because the wind was dead.

Will he come back again, or is he dead?
O! is he sleeping, my scarf round his head?

Or did they strangle him as he lay there,
With the long scarlet scarf I used to wear?

Only I pray thee, Lord, let him come here!
Both his soul and his body to me are most dear.

Dear Lord, that loves me, I wait to receive
Either body or spirit this wild Christmas-eve.

Through the floor shot up a lily red,
With a patch of earth from the land of the dead,
For he was strong in the land of the dead.

What matter that his cheeks were pale,
  His kind kiss'd lips all grey?
'O, love Louise, have you waited long?'
  'O, my lord Arthur, yea.'

What if his hair that brush'd her cheek
  Was stiff with frozen rime?
His eyes were grown quite blue again,
  As in the happy time.

'O, love Louise, this is the key
  Of the happy golden land!
O, sisters, cross the bridge with me,
  My eyes are full of sand.
What matter that I cannot see,
  If ye take me by the hand?'

And ever the great bell overhead,
And the tumbling seas mourn'd for the dead;
For their song ceased, and they were dead.

Golden Wings

Midways of a walled garden,
  In the happy poplar land,
  Did an ancient castle stand,
With an old knight for a warden.

Many scarlet bricks there were
   In its walls, and old grey stone;
   Over which red apples shone
At the right time of the year.

On the bricks the green moss grew,
   Yellow lichen on the stone,
   Over which red apples shone;
Little war that castle knew.

Deep green water fill'd the moat,
   Each side had a red-brick lip,
   Green and mossy with the drip
Of dew and rain; there was a boat

Of carven wood, with hangings green
   About the stern; it was great bliss
   For lovers to sit there and kiss
In the hot summer noons, not seen.

Across the moat the fresh west wind
   In very little ripples went;
   The way the heavy aspens bent
Towards it, was a thing to mind.

The painted drawbridge over it
   Went up and down with gilded chains,
   'Twas pleasant in the summer rains
Within the bridge-house there to sit.

There were five swans that ne'er did eat
   The water-weeds, for ladies came
   Each day, and young knights did the same,
And gave them cakes and bread for meat.

They had a house of painted wood,
   A red roof gold-spiked over it,
   Wherein upon their eggs to sit
Week after week; no drop of blood,

Drawn from men's bodies by sword-blows,
  Came ever there, or any tear;
  Most certainly from year to year
'Twas pleasant as a Provence rose.

The banners seem'd quite full of ease,
  That over the turret-roofs hung down;
  The battlements could get no frown
From the flower-moulded cornices.

Who walked in that garden there?
  Miles and Giles and Isabeau,
  Tall Jehane du Castel beau,
Alice of the golden hair,

Big Sir Gervaise, the good knight,
  Fair Ellayne le Violet,
  Mary, Constance fille de fay,
Many dames with footfall light.

Whosoever wander'd there,
  Whether it be dame or knight,
  Half of scarlet, half of white
Their raiment was; of roses fair

Each wore a garland on the head,
  At Ladies' Gard the way was so:
  Fair Jehane du Castel beau
Wore her wreath till it was dead.

Little joy she had of it,
  Of the raiment white and red,
  Or the garland on her head,
She had none with whom to sit

In the carven boat at noon;
  None the more did Jehane weep,
  She would only stand and keep
Saying, 'He will be here soon.'

71

Many times in the long day
 Miles and Giles and Gervaise past,
 Holding each some white hand fast,
Every time they heard her say:

'Summer cometh to an end,
 Undern cometh after noon;
 Golden wings will be here soon,
What if I some token send?'

Wherefore that night within the hall,
 With open mouth and open eyes,
 Like some one listening with surprise,
She sat before the sight of all.

Stoop'd down a little she sat there,
 With neck stretch'd out and chin thrown up,
 One hand around a golden cup;
And strangely with her fingers fair

She beat some tune upon the gold;
 The minstrels in the gallery
 Sung: 'Arthur, who will never die,
In Avallon he groweth old.'

And when the song was ended, she
 Rose and caught up her gown and ran;
 None stopp'd her eager face and wan
Of all that pleasant company.

Right so within her own chamber
 Upon her bed she sat; and drew
 Her breath in quick gasps; till she knew
That no man follow'd after her:

She took the garland from her head,
 Loosed all her hair, and let it lie
 Upon the coverlit; thereby
She laid the gown of white and red;

And she took off her scarlet shoon,
   And bared her feet; still more and more
   Her sweet face redden'd; evermore
She murmur'd; 'He will be here soon;

'Truly he cannot fail to know
   My tender body waits him here;
   And if he knows, I have no fear
For poor Jehane du Castel beau.'

She took a sword within her hand,
   Whose hilts were silver, and she sung,
   Somehow like this, wild words that rung
A long way over the moonlit land:

      Gold wings across the sea!
      Grey light from tree to tree,
      Gold hair beside my knee,
      I pray thee come to me,
      Gold wings!

             The water slips,
      The red-bill'd moorhen dips.
      Sweet kisses on red lips;
      Alas! the red rust grips,
      And the blood-red dagger rips,
      Yet, O knight, come to me!

      Are not my blue eyes sweet?
      The west wind from the wheat
      Blows cold across my feet;
      Is it not time to meet
      Gold wings across the sea?

      White swans on the green moat,
      Small feathers left afloat
      By the blue-painted boat;
      Swift running of the stoat;
      Sweet gurgling note by note
      Of sweet music.

                        O gold wings,
            Listen how gold hair sings,
            And the Ladies' Castle rings,
            Gold wings across the sea.

            I sit on a purple bed,
            Outside, the wall is red,
            Thereby the apple hangs,
            And the wasp, caught by the fangs,

            Dies in the autumn night,
            And the bat flits till light,
            And the love-crazed knight

            Kisses the long wet grass :
            The weary days pass, —
            Gold wings across the sea !

            Gold wings across the sea !
            Moonlight from tree to tree,
            Sweet hair laid on my knee,
            O, sweet knight, come to me !

            Gold wings, the short night slips,
            The white swan's long neck drips,
            I pray thee, kiss my lips,
            Gold wings across the sea.

        No answer through the moonlit night ;
            No answer in the cold grey dawn ;
            No answer when the shaven lawn
        Grew green, and all the roses bright.

        Her tired feet look'd cold and thin,
            Her lips were twitch'd, and wretched tears,
            Some, as she lay, roll'd past her ears,
        Some fell from off her quivering chin.

Her long throat, stretch'd to its full length,
　　Rose up and fell right brokenly;
　　As though the unhappy heart was nigh
Striving to break with all its strength.

And when she slipp'd from off the bed,
　　Her cramp'd feet would not hold her; she
　　Sank down and crept on hand and knee,
On the window-sill she laid her head.

There, with crooked arm upon the sill,
　　She look'd out, muttering dismally
　　'There is no sail upon the sea,
No pennon on the empty hill.

'I cannot stay here all alone,
　　Or meet their happy faces here,
　　And wretchedly I have no fear;
A little while, and I am gone.'

Therewith she rose upon her feet,
　　And totter'd; cold and misery
　　Still made the deep sobs come, till she
At last stretch'd out her fingers sweet,

And caught the great sword in her hand;
　　And, stealing down the silent stair,
　　Barefooted in the morning air,
And only in her smock, did stand

Upright upon the green lawn grass;
　　And hope grew in her as she said:
　　'I have thrown off the white and red,
And pray God it may come to pass

'I meet him; if ten years go by
　　Before I meet him; if, indeed,
　　Meanwhile both soul and body bleed,
Yet there is end of misery,

75

'And I have hope. He could not come,
  But I can go to him and show
  These new things I have got to know,
And make him speak, who has been dumb.'

O Jehane! the red morning sun
  Changed her white feet to glowing gold,
  Upon her smock, on crease and fold,
Changed that to gold which had been dun.

O Miles, and Giles, and Isabeau,
  Fair Ellayne le Violet,
  Mary, Constance fille de fay!
Where is Jehane du Castel beau?

O big Gervaise ride apace!
  Down to the hard yellow sand,
  Where the water meets the land.
This is Jehane by her face;

Why has she a broken sword?
  Mary! she is slain outright;
  Verily a piteous sight;
Take her up without a word!

Giles and Miles and Gervaise there,
  Ladies' Gard must meet the war;
  Whatsoever knights these are,
Man the walls withouten fear!

Axes to the apple-trees,
  Axes to the aspens tall!
  Barriers without the wall
May be lightly made of these.

O poor shivering Isabeau;
  Poor Ellayne le Violet,
  Bent with fear! we miss to-day
Brave Jehane du Castel beau.

O poor Mary, weeping so!
    Wretched Constance fille de fay!
    Verily we miss to-day
Fair Jehane du Castel beau.

The apples now grow green and sour
    Upon the mouldering castle-wall,
    Before they ripen there they fall:
There are no banners on the tower.

The draggled swans most eagerly eat
    The green weeds trailing in the moat;
    Inside the rotting leaky boat
You see a slain man's stiffen'd feet.

The Haystack in the Floods

Had she come all the way for this,
To part at last without a kiss?
Yea, had she borne the dirt and rain
That her own eyes might see him slain
Beside the haystack in the floods?

Along the dripping leafless woods,
The stirrup touching either shoe,
She rode astride as troopers do;
With kirtle kilted to her knee,
To which the mud splash'd wretchedly;
And the wet dripp'd from every tree
Upon her head and heavy hair,
And on her eyelids broad and fair;
The tears and rain ran down her face.

By fits and starts they rode apace,
And very often was his place
Far off from her; he had to ride
Ahead, to see what might betide

When the roads cross'd; and sometimes, when
There rose a murmuring from his men,
Had to turn back with promises;
Ah me! she had but little ease;
And often for pure doubt and dread
She sobb'd, made giddy in the head
By the swift riding; while, for cold,
Her slender fingers scarce could hold
The wet reins: yea, and scarcely, too,
She felt the foot within her shoe
Against the stirrup: all for this,
To part at last without a kiss
Beside the haystack in the floods.

For when they near'd that old soak'd hay,
They saw across the only way
That Judas, Godmar, and the three
Red running lions dismally
Grinn'd from his pennon, under which,
In one straight line along the ditch,
They counted thirty heads.

                                    So then,
While Robert turn'd round to his men,
She saw at once the wretched end,
And, stooping down, tried hard to rend
Her coif the wrong way from her head,
And hid her eyes; while Robert said:
'Nay, love, 'tis scarcely two to one,
At Poictiers where we made them run
So fast — why, sweet my love, good cheer,
The Gascon frontier is so near,
Nought after this.'

                              But, 'O,' she said,
'My God! my God! I have to tread
The long way back without you; then
The court at Paris; those six men;
The gratings of the Chatelet;

The swift Seine on some rainy day
Like this, and people standing by,
And laughing, while my weak hands try
To recollect how strong men swim.
All this, or else a life with him,
For which I should be damned at last,
Would God that this next hour were past!'

He answer'd not, but cried his cry,
'St. George for Marny!' cheerily;
And laid his hand upon her rein.
Alas! no man of all his train
Gave back that cheery cry again;
And, while for rage his thumb beat fast
Upon his sword-hilt, some one cast
About his neck a kerchief long,
And bound him.

             Then they went along
To Godmar; who said: 'Now, Jehane,
Your lover's life is on the wane
So fast, that, if this very hour
You yield not as my paramour,
He will not see the rain leave off —
Nay, keep your tongue from gibe and scoff,
Sir Robert, or I slay you now.'

She laid her hand upon her brow,
Then gazed upon the palm, as though
She thought her forehead bled, and — 'No.'
She said, and turn'd her head away,
As there were nothing else to say,
And everything were settled: red
Grew Godmar's face from chin to head:
'Jehane, on yonder hill there stands
My castle, guarding well my lands:
What hinders me from taking you,
And doing that I list to do

To your fair wilful body, while
Your knight lies dead?'

             A wicked smile
Wrinkled her face, her lips grew thin,
A long way out she thrust her chin:
'You know that I should strangle you
While you were sleeping; or bite through
Your throat, by God's help — ah!' she said,
'Lord Jesus, pity your poor maid!
For in such wise they hem me in,
I cannot choose but sin and sin,
Whatever happens: yet I think
They could not make me eat or drink,
And so should I just reach my rest.'
'Nay, if you do not my behest,
O Jehane! though I love you well,'
Said Godmar, 'would I fail to tell
All that I know.' 'Foul lies,' she said.
'Eh? lies my Jehane? by God's head,
At Paris folks would deem them true!
Do you know, Jehane, they cry for you,
"Jehane the brown! Jehane the brown!
Give us Jehane to burn or drown!" —
Eh — gag me, Robert! — sweet my friend,
This were indeed a piteous end
For those long fingers, and long feet,
And long neck, and smooth shoulders sweet;
An end that few men would forget
That saw it — So, an hour yet:
Consider, Jehane, which to take
Of life or death!'

            So, scarce awake,
Dismounting, did she leave that place,
And totter some yards: with her face
Turn'd upward to the sky she lay,
Her head on a wet heap of hay,

And fell asleep : and while she slept,
And did not dream, the minutes crept
Round to the twelve again ; but she,
Being waked at last, sigh'd quietly,
And strangely childlike came, and said :
'I will not.' Straightway Godmar's head,
As though it hung on strong wires, turn'd
Most sharply round, and his face burn'd.

For Robert — both his eyes were dry,
He could not weep, but gloomily
He seem'd to watch the rain ; yea, too,
His lips were firm ; he tried once more
To touch her lips ; she reach'd out, sore
And vain desire so tortured them,
The poor grey lips, and now the hem
Of his sleeve brush'd them.

                    With a start
Up Godmar rose, thrust them apart ;
From Robert's throat he loosed the bands
Of silk and mail ; with empty hands
Held out, she stood and gazed, and saw,
The long bright blade without a flaw
Glide out from Godmar's sheath, his hand
In Robert's hair ; she saw him bend
Back Robert's head ; she saw him send
The thin steel down ; the blow told well,
Right backward the knight Robert fell,
And moan'd as dogs do, being half dead,
Unwitting, as I deem : so then
Godmar turn'd grinning to his men,
Who ran, some five or six, and beat
His head to pieces at their feet.

Then Godmar turn'd again and said :
'So, Jehane, the first fitte is read !
   Take note, my lady, that your way

Lies backward to the Chatelet!'
She shook her head and gazed awhile
At her cold hands with a rueful smile,
As though this thing had made her mad.

This was the parting that they had
Beside the haystack in the floods.

Two Red Roses across the Moon

There was a lady lived in a hall,
Large in the eyes, and slim and tall;
And ever she sung from noon to noon,
Two red roses across the moon.

There was a knight came riding by
In early spring, when the roads were dry;
And he heard that lady sing at the noon,
Two red roses across the moon.

Yet none the more he stopp'd at all,
But he rode a-gallop past the hall;
And left that lady singing at noon,
Two red roses across the moon.

Because, forsooth, the battle was set,
And the scarlet and blue had got to be met,
He rode on the spur till the next warm noon: —
Two red roses across the moon.

But the battle was scatter'd from hill to hill,
From the windmill to the watermill;
And he said to himself, as it near'd the noon,
Two red roses across the moon.

You scarce could see for the scarlet and blue,
A golden helm or a golden shoe;
So he cried, as the fight grew thick at the noon,
Two red roses across the moon!

Verily then the gold bore through
The huddled spears of the scarlet and blue;
And they cried, as they cut them down at the noon,
Two red roses across the moon!

I trow he stopp'd when he rode again
By the hall, though draggled sore with the rain;
And his lips were pinch'd to kiss at the noon
Two red roses across the moon.

Under the may she stoop'd to the crown,
All was gold, there was nothing of brown;
And the horns blew up in the hall at noon,
Two red roses across the moon.

Riding Together

For many, many days together
    The wind blew steady from the East;
For many days hot grew the weather,
    About the time of our Lady's Feast.

For many days we rode together,
    Yet met we neither friend nor foe;
Hotter and clearer grew the weather,
    Steadily did the East wind blow.

We saw the trees in the hot, bright weather,
    Clear-cut, with shadows very black,
As freely we rode on together
    With helms unlaced and bridles slack.

And often, as we rode together,
  We, looking down the green-bank'd stream,
Saw flowers in the sunny weather,
  And saw the bubble-making bream.

And in the night lay down together,
  And hung above our heads the rood,
Or watch'd night-long in the dewy weather,
  The while the moon did watch the wood.

Our spears stood bright and thick together,
  Straight out the banners stream'd behind,
As we gallop'd on in the sunny weather,
  With faces turn'd towards the wind.

Down sank our threescore spears together,
  As thick we saw the pagans ride;
His eager face in the clear fresh weather,
  Shone out that last time by my side.

Up the sweep of the bridge we dash'd together,
  It rock'd to the crash of the meeting spears,
Down rain'd the buds of the dear spring weather,
  The elm-tree flowers fell like tears.

There, as we roll'd and writhed together,
  I threw my arms above my head,
For close by my side, in the lovely weather,
  I saw him reel and fall back dead.

I and the slayer met together,
  He waited the death-stroke there in his place,
With thoughts of death, in the lovely weather,
  Gapingly mazed at my madden'd face.

Madly I fought as we fought together;
  In vain: the little Christian band
The pagans drown'd, as in stormy weather,
  The river drowns low-lying land.

They bound my blood-stained hands together,
   They bound his corpse to nod by my side:
Then on we rode, in the bright March weather,
   With clash of cymbals did we ride.

We ride no more, no more together;
   My prison-bars are thick and strong,
I take no heed of any weather,
   The sweet Saints grant I live not long.

The Hollow Land

Christ keep the Hollow Land
   Through the sweet spring-tide,
When the apple-blossoms bless
   The lowly bent hill side.

Christ keep the Hollow Land
   All the summer-tide;
Still we cannot understand
   Where the waters glide;

Only dimly seeing them
   Coldly slipping through
Many green-lipp'd cavern mouths,
   Where the hills are blue.

Summer Dawn

Pray but one prayer for me 'twixt thy closed lips,
   Think but one thought of me up in the stars.
The summer night waneth, the morning light slips,
   Faint and grey 'twixt the leaves of the aspen, betwixt the
      cloud-bars,
That are patiently waiting there for the dawn:

Patient and colourless, though Heaven's gold
Waits to float through them along with the sun.
Far out in the meadows, above the young corn,
    The heavy elms wait, and restless and cold
The uneasy wind rises; the roses are dun;
Through the long twilight they pray for the dawn,
Round the lone house in the midst of the corn.
    Speak but one word to me over the corn,
    Over the tender, bow'd locks of the corn.

Out of *Scenes from the Fall of Troy*

i. HELEN ARMING PARIS

Troy: *on a lonely part of the walls*

PARIS

So, my sweet thing, a little tighter yet.
Look you, it must not rattle or some blow
Given at hazard on my knee-cap here
Would drive the thin edge in my foot. (*sighing*)
My sweet thing, shall I talk or hold my tongue?

HELEN

Shall I say, Paris, that my heart is faint,
And my head sick? I grow afraid of death:
The Gods are all against us, and some day
The long black ships rowed equal on each side
Shall throng the Trojan bay, and I shall walk
From off the green earth to the straining ship;
Cold Agamemnon with his sickly smile
Shall go before me, and behind shall go
My old chain Menelaus: we shall sit
Under the deck amid the oars, and hear
From day to day their wretched measured beat
Against the washing surges; they shall sit
There in that twilight, with their faces turned

Away from mine, and we shall say no word;
And I shall be too sick at heart to sing,
Though the rough dirt-grimed mariners may sing
Through all their weariness their rowing-song
Of Argo and the Golden Fleece, and Her
That made and marred them all in a short while,
As any potter might do with his clay,
Medea the Colchian. We shall come at last
To land in Greece, and all shall cry at me,
'See her who slew the sons of Priamus,
Who threw to earth that right fair town of Troy,
Who slew full many a mother's son of Greece!
See how she walks still like a Queen! By the Gods!
Is there no faggot for her false white limbs?
No sack, wherein, close sewn and crying out,
She may roll down the steep gulfs of the sea?
Is there no butcher's knife?'

PARIS

                    Nay hold, my love!
And let Greek butchers butcher their own lambs,
For you are ours: and let the sea-folk roll
Their own sea-calves in sack of woven sea-weed,
For you are ours: and let the beechen-wood
Bake bread for Greeks: seeing that you are ours.
Look Helen, hence upon our walls of stone,
Our great wet ditches where the carp and tench
In spite of arblasts and petrariae
Suck at the floating lilies all day long;
Look at the mighty barriers of fir-wood,
And look at Ilium rising over all,
Then at the few white tents and green log-huts
Of the Greek leaguer: listen too, my love
And you shall hear the muster of our men
Down in the streets, and marching toward the gates
Of many a captain. Ah! my sweet Helen,
Full many a day shall we kiss thus and thus
Before that last day when you kiss me dead,

An old man lying where the incense burns.

HELEN

Lips upon lips is surely a sweet game;
But I have ruined you, oh poor Paris,
My poor kind knight, who never for himself
Would look a yard before his sweet grey eyes;
Who taught me how to live, when long ago
I had forgotten that the world was fair
And I was fair: who made my lying down
Right peaceful to my tired heart and limbs,
Who made my waking sweet to rested eyes,
Who gave me joyful hours day by day.
In turn I give you this: no peace at all,
At best your weary anxiousness put off
So that it crushes not, pain and trouble, dear,
To you and all your kin; and at the worst —
O Paris, Paris, what care I for the Greeks?
They will not slay me, as I know full well,
And time will stay their babble and hard words.
Yea, I shall live a Queen while you lie slain —
But think of Troy with wolves about the streets,
Some yellow lion couched upon the place
Where first you called out, 'Troy, love! this is Troy!'
And men all shouted, 'Helen! the fair Dame!'
But on their skulls that lion shall look then
And bones of women that looked out at me
Calling out 'Helen!' — bones of young children
Born in the siege, who never knew of peace:
Fair, tall Andromache gone who knows where,
And Hector fallen dead among the spears,
One man to hundreds, when the rest are slain
And Troy is burning: yea good Helenus
Slain at his altar, and Cassandra mocked,
Used like a jester, while the Grecian wine
Stains Priam's golden cups: and Priam slain,
And Troilus slain before his withered hope
Can spring afresh: Deiphobus dead, slain,

88

Thrust in some ditch the salt sea sometimes fills
When wind and tide are high: Polyxena,
Younger than me and fairer she is now,
Sadder therefore and longer shall she live
As some man's slave— In what way, love Paris
Will they slay you, I wonder? will they call,
'Come Helen, come to this our sacrifice,
For Paris shall be slain at the sea's foot'?
Or will they wake me from my weeping sleep
Dangling your head above me by the hair,
Then all day long send women to dress me,
And scent my limbs, and comb my hair and bathe
My dull red eyelids till they grow stone-white,
Then set me at the feast among the wine
In Agamemnon's tent, to hear them tell
Long tales about the war, and hear them sing
Right in mine ears forgotten songs of Greece?

PARIS

Sweet, will you count our love an idle tale,
A thing the years take from us day by day,
A thing that was once but forgotten now?
Love, though indeed the bitter death may come,
And unclasp both my arms from round your neck,
Yet have I lived once. Helen, when I think
The fairest thing the Gods have made will sit
Hours together with her cheek laid on mine
And praises my poor doings, and looks pale
When from the mellay something scratched I come —
Say, lets me love her — why today, Helen,
I feel so light of heart with my great joy
That I can scarce be sober — shall I say,
Half jesting, half in earnest, as I take
Your fair long hand and kiss it, that our folk,
All Trojans, would be glad to die for this?
By God, Helen, but half I deem it true.

HELEN

    Do not believe it, Paris: bitterly
    Death comes to all, and they have their own wives,
    Own loves or children: Paris, you know not
    What death can do: pray God you curse me not
    When you leave off being happy — do you think
    We can be happy in the end, Paris?
    I shudder when I think of those fell men
    Who every day stand round about Troy Town
    And every night wipe the rust off their spears.
    They have no thoughts of pleasure or of love;
    Each day they rise to see the walls of Troy
    Still stand unbreached, and in the dead of night
    Awake or dreaming, still they think of it;
    Unspoken vows lie coiled about their hearts,
    Unspoken wrath is in their heavy hands,
    They are become mine enemies, yet still
    I am half grieved for their unspoken woes,
    And longings for the merry fields of Greece:
    They know themselves to be but ruined men
    Whatever happens — Doubt not they will win
    Their dreadful slow revenge at last, Paris.

PARIS

    Look you my love, it is not well to boast
    Of anything one has, for fear the Gods
    Should take it from us: yet I pray you think
    Of that great belt of Priam's sons, buckled
    By shining Hector the great clasp of all:
    The unfailing steadfast hearts of my brothers,
    Shall they not match the fierce-eyed gloomy Greeks?

HELEN

    O me! my brother Hector, kind and true,
    How sweet thou art for ever unto me!
    Yet sometime shall Achilles have his day:
    Better a live dog than a dead lion, dear.

PARIS

    Behold him coming, glancing with a smile
    Down on the Grecian tents.

HELEN

                  Is it farewell
    To both of you? Would I could weep for love!
    But little ever have I used wet eyes
    When hurt I have been. Where go you, sweet lords?

HECTOR

    The word is, each in arms we meet straightway
    In Priam's Hall, then out at gates go we;
    And goodly tilting shall the Trojan dames
    See from the walls: right thick the Greeks are set,
    And even now the stones begin to fall
    By the Scæan gates from their petrariae.
    Why Paris! you look brave in arms today.
    See you do well! Helen shall see your works.

                                             Helen falls

    Helen! fair Helen!

PARIS

              O my God! Hector,
    What may all this forbode? She said true now,
    She never wept: I never saw her weep;
    But now she lies full length upon the stones
    And terrible her weeping is to hear,
    And terribly the sobs take half her breath:

                               Kneeling by Helen
    For God's sake, Helen! will you kill me, love?

HELEN

    Go out and fight! I cannot speak with you,
    No, no, I cannot kiss you: go, Paris.

PARIS

I will not leave you, Helen, till you do.
Tell me what ails you?

HELEN

O, Paris, Paris!
Let me lie still and leave me!

HECTOR

Come, brother!
For time presses. 'Tis better too for her;
She will weep out her full, and go to sleep,
And wake up in your arms tonight smiling.

Exeunt

ii. [HECUBA'S SONG]

Yea, in the merry days of old
The sailors all grew overbold:
Whereof should days remembered be
That brought bitter ill to me?
Days agone I wore but gold,
Like a light town across the wold
Seen by stars, I shone out bright:
Many a slave was mine of right.

Ah but in the days of old
The Sea Kings were waxen bold,
The yellow sands ran red with blood,
The town burned up both brick and wood;
In their long-ship they carried me
And set me down by a strange sea:
None of the Gods remembered me.

Ah in the merry days of old
My garments were all made of gold,
Now have I but one poor gown
Woven of black wool and brown.

I draw water from the well,
I bind wood that the men fell :
Whoso willeth smiteth me,
An old woman by the sea.

iii. [HELEN'S ARMING SONG]*

Love, within the hawthorn brake
Pray you be merry for my sake
While I last, for who knoweth
What thing cometh after death.

Sweet, be long in growing old,
Life and love in age grow cold ;
Hold fast to life for who knoweth
What thing cometh after death.

Trouble must be kept afar
Therefore go I to the war.
Less trouble is there among spears
Than mid hard words about your ears.

Love me then my sweet and fair
And curse the folk that drive me there,
Kiss me sweet ! for who knoweth
What thing cometh after death.

iv. [DRINK ABOUT, FOR NIGHT DOTH GO]

Drink about, for night doth go,
By daylight grey hairs will show ;
Now from silver lamps doth fall
Golden light on gilded wall ;
Seize this hour while you may ;
Let it pass — there cometh day
When all things will turn to grey.

* A later version from *The Earthly Paradise* is printed on page 101.

Let me think about my love
Softer than pink-footed dove;
Nobly-born, and meek, and wise
As the guard of Paradise.
She would be a King's despair
From her golden-gleaming hair
To her silver feet so fair.

Who shall pray to Proserpine
For her? Juno, for her line?
Pallas, for that she is wise
As the guard of Paradise?
Venus, she that maketh fair,
For her golden-gleaming hair?
Or Diana, the full fleet,
For her sweet and silver feet?
Ah! these even, should they care
For us that die, must once despair;
Therefore are they made most fair.

Ah! yes, she shall lie alone
Underneath a carven stone.
Then be merry while ye may
For to each shall come a day
When no pleasure shall be brought,
When no friend can guess our thought,
When all that has been, shall be nought.

From the Upland to the Sea

Shall we wake one morn of spring,
Glad at heart of everything,
Yet pensive with the thought of eve?
Then the white house shall we leave,
Pass the wind-flowers and the bays,
Through the garth, and go our ways,

Wandering down among the meads
Till our very joyance needs
Rest at last; till we shall come
To that Sun-God's lonely home,
Lonely on the hillside grey,
Whence the sheep have gone away;
Lonely till the feast-time is,
When with prayer and praise of bliss,
Thither comes the country side.
There awhile shall we abide,
Sitting low down in the porch
By that image with the torch:
Thy one white hand laid upon
The black pillar that was won
From the far-off Indian mine;
And my hand nigh touching thine,
But not touching; and thy gown
Fair with spring-flowers cast adown
From thy bosom and thy brow.
There the south-west wind shall blow
Through thine hair to reach my cheek,
As thou sittest, nor mayst speak,
Nor mayst move the hand I kiss
For the very depth of bliss;
Nay, nor turn thine eyes to me.
Then desire of the great sea
Nigh enow, but all unheard,
In the hearts of us is stirred,
And we rise, we twain at last,
And the daffodils downcast,
Feel thy feet and we are gone
From the lonely Sun-Crowned one.
Then the meads fade at our back,
And the spring day 'gins to lack
That fresh hope that once it had;
But we twain grow yet more glad,
And apart no more may go
When the grassy slope and low

Dieth in the shingly sand :
Then we wander hand in hand
By the edges of the sea,
And I weary more for thee
Than if far apart we were,
With a space of desert drear
'Twixt thy lips and mine, O love !
Ah, my joy, my joy thereof !

From *The Earthly Paradise*

i. AN APOLOGY

Of Heaven or Hell I have no power to sing,
I cannot ease the burden of your fears,
Or make quick-coming death a little thing,
Or bring again the pleasure of past years,
Nor for my words shall ye forget your tears,
Or hope again for aught that I can say,
The idle singer of an empty day.

But rather, when aweary of your mirth,
From full hearts still unsatisfied ye sigh,
And, feeling kindly unto all the earth,
Grudge every minute as it passes by,
Made the more mindful that the sweet days die —
— Remember me a little then I pray,
The idle singer of an empty day.

The heavy trouble, the bewildering care
That weighs us down who live and earn our bread,
These idle verses have no power to bear ;
So let me sing of names remembered,
Because they, living not, can ne'er be dead,
Or long time take their memory quite away
From us poor singers of an empty day.

Dreamer of dreams, born out of my due time,
Why should I strive to set the crooked straight?
Let it suffice me that my murmuring rhyme
Beats with light wing against the ivory gate,
Telling a tale not too importunate
To those who in the sleepy region stay,
Lulled by the singer of an empty day.

Folk say, a wizard to a northern king
At Christmas-tide such wondrous things did show,
That through one window men beheld the spring,
And through another saw the summer glow,
And through a third the fruited vines a-row,
While still, unheard, but in its wonted way,
Piped the drear wind of that December day.

So with this Earthly Paradise it is,
If ye will read aright, and pardon me,
Who strive to build a shadowy isle of bliss
Midmost the beating of the steely sea,
Where tossed about all hearts of men must be;
Whose ravening monsters mighty men shall slay,
Not the poor singer of an empty day.

ii. [From THE WANDERERS]

Forget six counties overhung with smoke,
Forget the snorting steam and piston stroke,
Forget the spreading of the hideous town;
Think rather of the pack-horse on the down,
And dream of London, small, and white, and clean,
The clear Thames bordered by its gardens green;
Think, that below bridge the green lapping waves
Smite some few keels that bear Levantine staves,
Cut from the yew wood on the burnt-up hill,
And pointed jars that Greek hands toiled to fill,
And treasured scanty spice from some far sea,

Florence gold cloth, and Ypres napery,
And cloth of Bruges, and hogsheads of Guienne;
While nigh the thronged wharf Geoffrey Chaucer's pen
Moves over bills of lading — mid such times
Shall dwell the hollow puppets of my rhymes.

iii. SONG [O DWELLERS ON THE LOVELY EARTH]

O dwellers on the lovely earth,
Why will ye break your rest and mirth
To weary us with fruitless prayer;
Why will ye toil and take such care
For children's children yet unborn,
And garner store of strife and scorn
To gain a scarce-remembered name,
Cumbered with lies and soiled with shame?
And if the gods care not for you,
What is this folly ye must do
To win some mortal's feeble heart?
O fools! when each man plays his part,
And heeds his fellow little more
Than these blue waves that kiss the shore
Take heed of how the daisies grow.
O fools! and if ye could but know
How fair a world to you is given.

O brooder on the hills of heaven,
When for my sin thou drav'st me forth,
Hadst thou forgot what this was worth,
Thine hand had made? The tears of men,
The death of threescore years and ten,
The trembling of the timorous race —
Had these things so bedimmed the place
Thine own hand made, thou couldst not know
To what a heaven the earth might grow
If fear beneath the earth were laid,
If hope failed not, nor love decayed.

O love, this morn when the sweet nightingale
Had so long finished all he had to say,
That thou hadst slept, and sleep had told his tale;
And midst a peaceful dream had stolen away
In fragrant dawning of the first of May,
Didst thou see aught? didst thou hear voices sing
Ere to the risen sun the bells 'gan ring?

For then methought the Lord of Love went by
To take possession of his flowery throne,
Ringed round with maids, and youths, and minstrelsy;
A little while I sighed to find him gone,
A little while the dawning was alone,
And the light gathered; then I held my breath,
And shuddered at the sight of Eld and Death.

Alas! Love passed me in the twilight dun,
His music hushed the wakening ousel's song;
But on these twain shone out the golden sun,
And o'er their heads the brown bird's tune was strong,
As shivering, 'twixt the trees they stole along;
None noted aught their noiseless passing by,
The world had quite forgotten it must die.

v. [From PYGMALION AND THE IMAGE]

August had not gone by, though now was stored
In the sweet-smelling granaries all the hoard
Of golden corn; the land had made her gain,
And winter should howl round her doors in vain.
But o'er the same fields grey now and forlorn
The old men sat and heard the swineherd's horn,
Far off across the stubble, when the day
At end of harvest-tide was sad and grey;

And rain was in the wind's voice, as it swept
Along the hedges where the lone quail crept,
Beneath the chattering of the restless pie.
The fruit-hung branches moved, and suddenly
The trembling apples smote the dewless grass,
And all the year to autumn-tide did pass.

vi. SEPTEMBER*

O come at last, to whom the spring-tide's hope
Looked for through blossoms, what hast thou for me?
Green grows the grass upon the dewy slope
Beneath thy gold-hung, grey-leaved apple-tree
Moveless, e'en as the autumn fain would be
That shades its sad eyes from the rising sun
And weeps at eve because the day is done.

What vision wilt thou give me, autumn morn,
To make thy pensive sweetness more complete?
What tale, ne'er to be told, of folk unborn?
What images of grey-clad damsels sweet
Shall cross thy sward with dainty noiseless feet?
What nameless shamefast longings made alive,
Soft-eyed September, will thy sad heart give?

Look long, O longing eyes, and look in vain!
Strain idly, aching heart, and yet be wise,
And hope no more for things to come again
That thou beheldest once with careless eyes!
Like a new-wakened man thou art, who tries
To dream again the dream that made him glad
When in his arms his loving love he had.

* Compare 'Sad-eyed and Soft and Grey', page 109.

vii. SONG [In the white-flowered hawthorn brake]

HÆC

In the white-flowered hawthorn brake,
Love, be merry for my sake;
Twine the blossoms in my hair,
Kiss me where I am most fair —
Kiss me, love! for who knoweth
What thing cometh after death?

ILLE

Nay, the garlanded gold hair
Hides thee where thou art most fair;
Hides the rose-tinged hills of snow —
Ah, sweet love, I have thee now!
Kiss me, love! for who knoweth
What thing cometh after death?

HÆC

Shall we weep for a dead day,
Or set Sorrow in our way?
Hidden by my golden hair,
Wilt thou weep that sweet days wear?
Kiss me, love! for who knoweth
What thing cometh after death?

ILLE

Weep, O Love, the days that flit,
Now, while I can feel thy breath;
Then may I remember it
Sad and old, and near my death.
Kiss me, love! for who knoweth
What thing cometh after death?

Outlanders, whence come ye last?
The snow in the street and the wind on the door.
Through what green seas and great have ye passed?
Minstrels and maids, stand forth on the floor.

From far away, O masters mine,
The snow in the street and the wind on the door.
We come to bear you goodly wine,
Minstrels and maids, stand forth on the floor

From far away we come to you,
The snow in the street and the wind on the door.
To tell of great tidings strange and true.
Minstrels and maids, stand forth on the floor.

News, news of the Trinity,
The snow in the street and the wind on the door.
And Mary and Joseph from over the sea!
Minstrels and maids, stand forth on the floor.

For as we wandered far and wide,
The snow in the street and the wind on the door.
What hap do ye deem there should us betide!
Minstrels and maids, stand forth on the floor.

Under a bent when the night was deep,
The snow in the street and the wind on the door.
There lay three shepherds tending their sheep.
Minstrels and maids, stand forth on the floor.

'O ye shepherds, what have ye seen,
The snow in the street and the wind on the door.
To slay your sorrow, and heal your teen?'
Minstrels and maids, stand forth on the floor.

'In an ox-stall this night we saw,
   The snow in the street and the wind on the door.
A babe and a maid without a flaw.
   Minstrels and maids, stand forth on the floor.

'There was an old man there beside,
   The snow in the street and the wind on the door.
His hair was white and his hood was wide.
   Minstrels and maids, stand forth on the floor.

'And as we gazed this thing upon,
   The snow in the street and the wind on the door.
Those twain knelt down to the Little One.
   Minstrels and maids, stand forth on the floor.

'And a marvellous song we straight did hear,
   The snow in the street and the wind on the door.
That slew our sorrow and healed our care.'
   Minstrels and maids, stand forth on the floor.

News of a fair and a marvellous thing,
   The snow in the street and the wind on the door.
Nowell, nowell, nowell, we sing!
   Minstrels and maids, stand forth on the floor.

ix. OCTOBER

O love, turn from the unchanging sea, and gaze
Down these grey slopes upon the year grown old,
A-dying mid the autumn-scented haze,
That hangeth o'er the hollow in the wold,
Where the wind-bitten ancient elms enfold
Grey church, long barn, orchard, and red-roofed stead,
Wrought in dead days for men a long while dead.

Come down, O love; may not our hands still **meet,**
Since still we live to-day, forgetting June,
Forgetting May, deeming October sweet —
— O hearken, hearken! through the afternoon,
The grey tower sings a strange old tinkling tune!
Sweet, sweet, and sad, the toiling year's last breath,
Too satiate of life to strive with death.

And we too — will it not be soft and kind,
That rest from life, from patience and from pain;
That rest from bliss we know not when we find;
That rest from Love which ne'er the end can gain? —
— Hark, how the tune swells, that erewhile did wane!
Look up, love! — ah, cling close and never move!
How can I have enough of life and love?

X. NOVEMBER

Are thine eyes weary? is thy heart too sick
To struggle any more with doubt and thought,
Whose formless veil draws darkening now and thick
Across thee, e'en as smoke-tinged mist-wreaths brought
Down a fair dale to make it blind and nought?
Art thou so weary that no world there seems
Beyond these four walls, hung with pain and dreams?

Look out upon the real world, where the moon,
Half-way 'twixt root and crown of these high trees,
Turns the dead midnight into dreamy noon,
Silent and full of wonders, for the breeze
Died at the sunset, and no images,
No hopes of day, are left in sky or earth —
Is it not fair, and of most wondrous worth?

Yea, I have looked, and seen November there;
The changeless seal of change it seemed to be,
Fair death of things that, living once, were fair;

Bright sign of loneliness too great for me,
Strange image of the dread eternity,
In whose void patience how can these have part,
These outstretched feverish hands, this restless heart?

xi. [SONG, from THE HILL OF VENUS]

Before our lady came on earth
Little there was of joy or mirth;
About the borders of the sea
The sea-folk wandered heavily;
About the wintry river side
The weary fishers would abide.

Alone within the weaving-room
The girls would sit before the loom,
And sing no song, and play no play;
Alone from dawn to hot mid-day,
From mid-day unto evening,
The men afield would work, nor sing,
'Mid weary thoughts of man and God,
Before thy feet the wet ways trod.

Unkissed the merchant bore his care,
Unkissed the knights went out to war,
Unkissed the mariner came home,
Unkissed the minstrel men did roam,

Or in the stream the maids would stare,
Nor know why they were made so fair;
Their yellow locks, their bosoms white,
Their limbs well wrought for all delight,
Seemed foolish things that waited death,
As hopeless as the flowers beneath
The weariness of unkissed feet:
No life was bitter then, or sweet.

Therefore, O Venus, well may we
Praise the green ridges of the sea
O'er which, upon a happy day,
Thou cam'st to take our shame away.
Well may we praise the curdling foam
Amidst the which thy feet did bloom,
Flowers of the gods; the yellow sand
They kissed atwixt the sea and land;
The bee-beset ripe-seeded grass,
Through which thy fine limbs first did pass;
The purple-dusted butterfly,
First blown against thy quivering thigh;
The first red rose that touched thy side,
And over-blown and fainting died;
The flickering of the orange shade,
Where first in sleep thy limbs were laid;
The happy day's sweet life and death,
Whose air first caught thy balmy breath —
Yea, all these things well praised may be,
But with what words shall we praise thee —
O Venus, O thou love alive,
Born to give peace to souls that strive?

xii. JANUARY

From this dull rainy undersky and low,
This murky ending of a leaden day,
That never knew the sun, this half-thawed snow.
These tossing black boughs faint against the grey
Of gathering night, thou turnest, dear, away
Silent, but with thy scarce-seen kindly smile
Sent through the dusk my longing to beguile.

There, the lights gleam, and all is dark without!
And in the sudden change our eyes meet dazed —
O look, love, look again! the veil of doubt
Just for one flash, past counting, then was raised!

O eyes of heaven, as clear thy sweet soul blazed
On mine a moment! O come back again
Strange rest and dear amid the long dull pain!

Nay, nay, gone by! though there she sitteth still,
With wide grey eyes so frank and fathomless —
Be patient, heart, thy days they yet shall fill
With utter rest — Yea, now thy pain they bless,
And feed thy last hope of the world's redress —
O unseen hurrying rack! O wailing wind!
What rest and where go ye this night to find?

xiii. FEBRUARY

Noon — and the north-west sweeps the empty road,
The rain-washed fields from hedge to hedge are bare;
Beneath the leafless elms some hind's abode
Looks small and void, and no smoke meets the air
From its poor hearth: one lonely rook doth dare
The gale, and beats above the unseen corn,
Then turns, and whirling down the wind is borne.

Shall it not hap that on some dawn of May
Thou shalt awake, and, thinking of days dead,
See nothing clear but this same dreary day,
Of all the days that have passed o'er thine head?
Shalt thou not wonder, looking from thy bed,
Through green leaves on the windless east a-fire,
That this day too thine heart doth still desire?

Shalt thou not wonder that it liveth yet,
The useless hope, the useless craving pain,
That made thy face, that lonely noontide, wet
With more than beating of the chilly rain?
Shalt thou not hope for joy new born again,
Since no grief ever born can ever die
Through changeless change of seasons passing by?

Thunder in the Garden

When the boughs of the garden hang heavy with rain
And the blackbird reneweth his song,
And the thunder departing yet rolleth again,
I remember the ending of wrong.

When the day that was dusk while his death was aloof
Is ending wide-gleaming and strange
For the clearness of all things beneath the world's roof,
I call back the wild chance and the change.

For once we twain sat through the hot afternoon
While the rain held aloof for a while,
Till she, the soft-clad, for the glory of June
Changed all with the change of her smile.

For her smile was of longing, no longer of glee,
And her fingers, entwined with mine own,
With caresses unquiet sought kindness of me
For the gift that I never had known.

Then down rushed the rain, and the voice of the thunder
Smote dumb all the sound of the street,
And I to myself was grown nought but a wonder,
As she leaned down my kisses to meet.

That she craved for my lips that had craved her so often,
And the hand that had trembled to touch,
That the tears filled her eyes I had hoped not to soften
In this world was a marvel too much.

It was dusk 'mid the thunder, dusk e'en as the night,
When first brake out our love like the storm,
But no night-hour was it, and back came the light
While our hands with each other were warm.

And her smile killed with kisses, came back as at first
As she rose up and led me along,
And out to the garden, where nought was athirst,
And the blackbird renewing his song.

Earth's fragrance went with her, as in the wet grass,
Her feet little hidden were set;
She bent down her head, 'neath the roses to pass,
And her arm with the lily was wet.

In the garden we wandered while day waned apace
And the thunder was dying aloof;
Till the moon o'er the minster-wall lifted his face,
And grey gleamed out the lead of the roof.

Then we turned from the blossoms, and cold were they grown:
In the trees the wind westering moved;
Till over the threshold back fluttered her gown,
And in the dark house was I loved.

Sad-Eyed and Soft and Grey*

Sad-eyed and soft and grey thou art, O morn!
    Across the long grass of the marshy plain
    Thy west wind whispers of the coming rain,
Thy lark forgets that May is grown forlorn
Above the lush blades of the springing corn,
    Thy thrush within the high elms strives in vain
    To store up tales of spring for summer's pain —
Vain day, why wert thou from the dark night born?

O many-voiced strange morn, why must thou break
    With vain desire the softness of my dream
    Where she and I alone on earth did seem?
How hadst thou heart from me that land to take
Wherein she wandered softly for my sake
    And I and she no harm of love might deem?

* Compare the September lines from *The Earthly Paradise,* page 100.

Rhyme Slayeth Shame

If as I come unto her she might hear,
    If words might reach her when from her I go,
    Then speech a little of my heart might show,
Because indeed nor joy nor grief nor fear
Silence my love; but her gray eyes and clear,
    Truer than truth, pierce through my weal and woe;
    The world fades with its woods, and naught I know
But that my changed life to My Life is near.

Go, then, poor rhymes, who know my heart indeed,
    And sing to her the words I cannot say, —
    That Love has slain Time, and knows no today
And no tomorrow; tell her of my need,
And how I follow where her footsteps lead,
    Until the veil of speech death draws away.

May Grown A-Cold

O certainly, no month this is but May!
    Sweet earth and sky, sweet birds of happy song,
    Do make thee happy now, and thou art strong,
And many a tear thy love shall wipe away
And make the dark night merrier than the day,
    Straighten the crooked paths and right the wrong,
    And tangle bliss so that it tarry long.
Go cry aloud the hope the Heavens do say!

Nay what is this? and wherefore lingerest thou?
    Why sayest thou the sky is hard as stone?
    Why sayest thou the thrushes sob and moan?
Why sayest thou the east tears bloom and bough?
Why seem the sons of man so hopeless now?
    Thy love is gone, poor wretch, thou art alone!

Song

'Twas one little word that wrought it,
One sweet pang of pleasure bought it;
Long 'twixt heart and lips it hung
Till too sore the heart was wrung,
Till no more the lips might bear
To be parted, yet so near —
Then the darkness closed around me
And the bitter waking found me
Half forgotten, unforgiven and alone.

Hearken: nigher still and nigher
Had we grown, methought my fire
Woke in her some hidden flame
And the rags of pride and shame
She seemed casting from her heart,
And the dull days seemed to part;
Then I cried out, Ah, I move thee
And thou knowest that I love thee —
— Half forgotten, unforgiven and alone.

Yea, it pleased her to behold me
Mocked by tales that love had told me,
Mocked by tales and mocked by eyes,
Wells of loving mysteries;
Mocked by eyes and mocked by speech
Till I deemed I might beseech
For one word, that scarcely speaking
She would snatch from me that waking,
Half forgotten, unforgiven and alone.

All is done — no other greeting,
No more sweet tormenting meeting,
No more sight of smile or tear,
No more bliss shall draw anear
Hand in hand with sister pain —
Scarce a longing vague and vain —

No more speech till all is over
Twixt the well-beloved and lover
Half forgotten, unforgiven and alone.

Why Dost Thou Struggle

Why dost thou struggle, strive for victory
Over my heart that loveth thine so well?
When Death shall one day have its will of thee
And to deaf ears thy triumph thou must tell.

Unto deaf ears or unto such as know
The hearts of dead and living wilt thou say :
A childish heart there loved me once, and lo
I took his love and cast his love away.

A childish greedy heart ! yet still he clung
So close to me that much he pleased my pride
And soothed a sorrow that about me hung
With glimpses of his love unsatisfied —

And soothed my sorrow — but time soothed it too
Though ever did its aching fill my heart
To which the foolish child still closer drew
Thinking in all I was to have a part.

But now my heart grown silent of its grief
Saw more than kindness in his hungry eyes :
But I must wear a mask of false belief
And feign that nought I know his miseries.

I wore a mask, because though certainly
I loved him not, yet was there something soft
And sweet to have him ever loving me :
Belike it is I well-nigh loved him oft —

Nigh loved him oft, and needs must grant to him
Some kindness out of all he asked of me
And hoped his love would still hang vague and dim
About my life like half-heard melody.

He knew my heart and over-well knew this
And strove, poor soul, to pleasure me herein;
But yet what might he do some doubtful kiss
Some word, some look might give him hope to win.

Poor hope, poor soul, for he again would come
Thinking to gain yet one more golden step
Toward Love's shrine, and lo the kind speech dumb,
The kind look gone, no love upon my lip —

Yea gone, yet not my fault, I knew of love
But my love and not his; how could I tell
That such blind passion in him I should move?
Behold I have loved faithfully and well;

Love of my love so deep and measureless
O lords of the new world this too ye know

(unfinished)

Fair Weather and Foul

Speak nought, move not, but listen, the sky is full of gold,
No ripple on the river, no stir in field or fold,
All gleams but nought doth glisten, but the far-off unseen sea.

Forget days past, heart broken, put all memory by!
No grief on the green hill-side, no pity in the sky,
Joy that may not be spoken fills mead and flower and tree.

Look not, they will not heed thee, speak not, they will not hear,
Pray not, they have no bounty, curse not, they may not fear,
Cower down, they will not heed thee; long-lived the world shall be.

Hang down thine head and hearken, for the bright eve mocks thee
    still:
Night trippeth on the twilight, but the summer hath no will
For woes of thine to darken, and the moon hath left the sea.

Hope not to tell thy story in the rest of grey-eyed morn,
In the dawn grown grey and rainy, for the thrush ere day is born
Shall be singing to the glory of the day-star mocking thee.

Be silent, worn and weary, till their tyranny is past,
For the summer joy shall darken, and the wind wail low at last,
And the drifting rack and dreary shall be kind to hear and see.

Thou shalt remember sorrow, thou shalt tell all thy tale
When the rain fills up the valley, and the trees amid their wail
Think far beyond tomorrow, and the sun that yet shall be.

Hill-side and vineyard hidden, and the river running rough,
Toward the flood that meets the northlands, shall be rest for thee
    enough
For thy tears to fall unbidden, for thy memory to go free.

Rest then, when all moans round thee, and no fair sunlitten lie
Maketh light of sorrow underneath a brazen sky,
And the tuneful woe hath found thee, over land and over sea.

From *The Story of Sigurd the Volsung and The Fall of the Niblungs*

Now Sigurd eats of the heart that once in the Dwarf-king lay,
The hoard of the wisdom begrudged, the might of the earlier day,
Then wise of heart was he waxen, but longing in him grew
To sow the seed he had gotten, and till the field he knew.
So he leapeth aback of Greyfell, and rideth the desert bare,
And the hollow slot of Fafnir, that led to the Serpent's lair.
Then long he rode adown it, and the ernes flew overhead,
And tidings great and glorious of that Treasure of old they said.
So far o'er the waste he wended, and when the night was come
He saw the earth-old dwelling, the dread Gold wallower's home:
On the skirts of the Heath it was builded by a tumbled stony bent;
High went that house to the heavens, down 'neath the earth it
    went.
Of unwrought iron fashioned for the heart of a greedy king:
'Twas a mountain, blind without, and within was its plenishing
But the Hoard of Andvari the ancient, and the sleeping Curse
    unseen,
The Gold of the Gods that spared not and the greedy that have
    been.

Through the door strode Sigurd the Volsung, and the grey moon
    and the sword
Fell in on the tawny gold-heaps of the ancient hapless Hoard:
Gold gear of hosts unburied, and the coin of cities dead,
Great spoil of the ages of battle, lay there on the Serpent's bed:
Huge blocks from the mid-earth quarried, where none but the
    Dwarfs have mined,
Wide sands of the golden rivers no foot of man may find
Lay 'neath the spoils of the mighty and the ruddy rings of yore:
But amidst was the Helm of Aweing that the Fear of earth-folk bore,
And there gleamed a wonder beside it, the Hauberk all of gold,

Whose like is not in the heavens nor has earth of its fellow told:
There Sigurd seeth moreover Andvari's Ring of Gain,
The hope of Loki's finger, the Ransom's utmost grain;
For it shone on the midmost gold-heap like the first star set in the
    sky
In the yellow space of even when moon-rise draweth anigh.
Then laughed the Son of Sigmund, and stooped to the golden land
And gathered the first of the harvest and set it on his hand;
And he did on the Helm of Aweing, and the Hauberk all of gold,
Whose like is not on the heavens nor has earth of its fellow told:
Then he praised the day of the Volsungs amid the yellow light,
And he set his hand to the labour and put forth his kingly might;
He dragged forth gold to the moon, on the desert's face he laid
The innermost earth's adornment, and rings for the nameless made;
He toiled and loaded Greyfell, and the Volsung armour rang
Mid the yellow bed of the Serpent: but without the eagles sang:

'Bind the red rings, O Sigurd! let the gold shine free and clear!
For what hath the Son of the Volsungs the ancient Curse to fear?'

'Bind the red rings, O Sigurd! for thy tale is well begun,
And the world shall be good and gladdened by the Gold lit up by
    the sun.'

'Bind the red rings, O Sigurd! and gladden all thine heart!
For the world shall make thee merry ere thou and she depart.'

'Bind the red rings, O Sigurd! for the ways go green below,
Go green to the dwelling of Kings, and the halls that the Queen-
    folk know.'

'Bind the red rings, O Sigurd! for what is there bides by the way,
Save the joy of folk to awaken, and the dawn of the merry day?'

'Bind the red rings, O Sigurd! for the strife awaits thine hand,
And a plenteous war-field's reaping, and the praise of many a
    land.'

'Bind the red rings, O Sigurd! But how shall storehouse hold
That glory of thy winning and the tidings to be told?'

Now the moon was dead, and the star-worlds were great on the
    heavenly plain,
When the steed was fully laden; then Sigurd taketh the rein
And turns to the ruined rock-wall that the lair was built beneath,
For there he deemed was the gate and the door of the Glittering
    Heath,
But not a whit moved Greyfell for aught that the King might do;
Then Sigurd pondered a while, till the heart of the beast he knew,
And clad in all his war-gear he leaped to the saddle-stead,
And with pride and mirth neighed Greyfell and tossed aloft his
    head,
And sprang unspurred o'er the waste, and light and swift he went,
And breasted the broken rampart, the stony tumbled bent;
And over the brow he clomb, and there beyond was the world,
A place of many mountains and great crags together hurled.
So down to the west he wendeth, and goeth swift and light,
And the stars are beginning to wane, and the day is mingled with
    night;
Full fain was the sun to arise and look on the Gold set free,
And the Dwarf-wrought rings of the Treasure and the gifts from
    the floor of the sea.

ii. HOW SIGURD AWOKE BRYNHILD UPON
HINDFELL

By long roads rideth Sigurd amidst that world of stone,
And somewhat south he turneth, for he would not be alone,
But longs for the dwellings of man-folk, and the kingly people's
    speech,
And the days of the glee and the joyance, where men laugh each to
    each.
But still the desert endureth, and afar must Greyfell fare
From the wrack of the Glittering Heath, and Fafnir's golden lair.

Long Sigurd rideth the waste, when, lo, on a morning of day
From out of the tangled crag-walls, amidst the cloud-land grey
Comes up a mighty mountain, and it is as though there burns
A torch amidst of its cloud-wreath; so thither Sigurd turns,
For he deems indeed from its topmost to look on the best of the
 earth;
And Greyfell neigheth beneath him, and his heart is full of mirth.

So he rideth higher and higher, and the light grows great and
 strange,
And forth from the clouds it flickers, till at noon they gather and
 change,
And settle thick on the mountain, and hide its head from sight;
But the winds in a while are awakened, and day bettereth ere the
 night,
And, lifted a measureless mass o'er the desert crag-walls high,
Cloudless the mountain riseth against the sunset sky,
The sea of the sun grown golden, as it ebbs from the day's desire;
And the light that afar was a torch is grown a river of fire,
And the mountain is black above it, and below is it dark and
 dun;
And there is the head of Hindfell as an island in the sun.

Night falls but yet rides Sigurd, and hath no thought of rest,
For he longs to climb that rock-world and behold the earth at its
 best;
But now mid the maze of the foot-hills he seeth the light no more,
And the stars are lovely and gleaming on the lightless heavenly
 floor.
So up and up he wendeth till the night is wearing thin;
And he rideth a rift of the mountain, and all is dark therein,
Till the stars are dimmed by dawning and the wakening world is
 cold;
Then afar in the upper rock-wall a breach doth he behold,
And a flood of light poured inward the doubtful dawning blinds:
So swift he rideth thither and the mouth of the breach he finds,
And sitteth awhile on Greyfell on the marvellous thing to gaze:
For lo, the side of Hindfell enwrapped by the fervent blaze,

And nought 'twixt earth and heaven save a world of flickering
flame,
And a hurrying shifting tangle, where the dark rents went and
came.

Great groweth the heart of Sigurd with uttermost desire,
And he crieth kind to Greyfell, and they hasten up, and nigher,
Till he draweth rein in the dawning on the face of Hindfell's steep:
But who shall heed the dawning where the tongues of that wildfire
leap?
For they weave a wavering wall, that driveth over the heaven
The wind that is born within it; nor ever aside is it driven
By the mightiest wind of the waste, and the rain-flood amidst it is
nought;
And no wayfarer's door and no window the hand of its builder
hath wrought
But thereon is the Volsung smiling as its breath uplifteth his hair,
And his eyes shine bright with its image, and his mail gleams
white and fair,
And his war-helm pictures the heavens and the waning stars
behind:
But his neck is Greyfell stretching to snuff at the flame-wall blind,
And his cloudy flank upheaveth, and tinkleth the knitted mail,
And the gold of the uttermost waters is waxen wan and pale.

Now Sigurd turns in his saddle, and the hilt of the Wrath he
shifts,
And draws a girth the tighter; then the gathered reins he lifts,
And crieth aloud to Greyfell, and rides at the wildfire's heart;
But the white wall wavers before him and the flame-flood rusheth
apart,
And high o'er his head it riseth, and wide and wild is its roar
As it beareth the mighty tidings to the very heavenly floor:
But he rideth through its roaring as the warrior rides the rye,
When it bows with the wind of summer and the hid spears draw
anigh.
The white flame licks his raiment and sweeps through Greyfell's
mane,

And bathes both hands of Sigurd and the hilts of Fafnir's bane,
And winds about his war-helm and mingles with his hair,
But nought his raiment dusketh or dims his glittering gear;
Then it fails and fades and darkens till all seems left behind,
And dawn and the blaze is swallowed in mid-mirk stark and
    blind.

But forth a little further and a little further on
And all is calm about him, and he sees the scorched earth wan
Beneath a glimmering twilight, and he turns his conquering eyes,
And a ring of pale slaked ashes on the side of Hindfell lies;
And the world of waste is beyond it; and all is hushed and grey,
And the new-risen moon is a-paleing, and the stars grow faint with
    day.

Then Sigurd looked before him and a Shield-burg there he saw,
A wall of the tiles of Odin wrought clear without a flaw,
The gold by the silver gleaming, and the ruddy by the white;
And the blazonings of their glory were done upon them bright,
As of dear things wrought for the war-lords new come to Odin's
    hall.
Piled high aloft to the heavens uprose that battle-wall,
And far o'er the topmost shield-rim for a banner of fame there hung
A glorious golden buckler; and against the staff it rung
As the earliest wind of dawning uprose on Hindfell's face
And the light from the yellowing east beamed soft on the shielded
    place.

But the Wrath cried out in answer as Sigurd leapt adown
To the wasted soil of the desert by that rampart of renown;
He looked but little beneath it, and the dwelling of God it seemed,
As against its gleaming silence the eager Sigurd gleamed:
He draweth not sword from scabbard, as the wall he wendeth
    around,
And it is but the wind and Sigurd that wakeneth any sound:
But, lo, to the gate he cometh, and the doors are open wide,
And no warder the way withstandeth, and no earls by the threshold
    abide

So he stands awhile and marvels; then the baleful light of the
    Wrath
Gleams bare in his ready hand as he wendeth the inward path:
For he doubteth some guile of the Gods, or perchance some Dwarf-
    king's snare,
Or a mock of the Giant people that shall fade in the morning air:
But he getteth him in and gazeth; and a wall doth he behold,
And the ruddy set by the white, and the silver by the gold;
But within the garth that it girdeth no work of man is set,
But the utmost head of Hindfell ariseth higher yet;
And below in the very midmost is a Giant-fashioned mound,
Piled high as the rims of the Shield-burg above the level ground;
And there, on that mound of the Giants, o'er the wilderness forlorn
A pale grey image lieth, and gleameth in the morn.

So there was Sigurd alone; and he went from the shielded door,
And aloft in the desert of wonder the Light of the Branstock he
    bore;
And he set his face to the earth-mound, and beheld the image
    wan,
And the dawn was growing about it; and, lo, the shape of a man
Set forth to the eyeless desert on the tower-top of the world,
High o'er the cloud-wrought castle whence the windy bolts are
    hurled.

Now he comes to the mound and climbs it, and will see if the man
    be dead,
Some King of the days forgotten laid there with crownèd head,
Or the frame of a God, it may be, that in heaven hath changed his
    life,
Or some glorious heart belovèd, God-rapt from the earthly strife:
Now over the body he standeth, and seeth it shapen fair,
And clad from head to foot-sole in pale grey-glittering gear,
In a hauberk wrought as straitly as though to the flesh it were
    grown:
But a great helm hideth the head and is girt with a glittering crown.

So thereby he stoopeth and kneeleth, for he deems it were good
  indeed
If the breath of life abide there and the speech to help at need;
And as sweet as the summer wind from a garden under the sun
Cometh forth on the topmost Hindfell the breath of that sleeping-
  one.
Then he saith he will look on the face, if it bear him love or hate,
Or the bonds for his life's constraining, or the sundering doom of
  fate.
So he draweth the helm from the head, and, lo, the brow snow-
  white,
And the smooth unfurrowed cheeks, and the wise lips breathing
  light;
And the face of a woman it is, and the fairest that ever was born,
Shown forth to the empty heavens and the desert world forlorn:
But he looketh, and loveth her sore, and he longeth her spirit to
  move,
And awaken her heart to the world, that she may behold him and
  love.
And he toucheth her breast and her hands, and he loveth her
  passing sore;
And he saith: 'Awake! I am Sigurd;' but she moveth never the
  more.
Then he looked on his bare bright blade, and he said: 'Thou —
  what wilt thou do?
For indeed as I came by the war-garth thy voice of desire I knew.'
Bright burnt the pale blue edges for the sunrise drew anear,
And the rims of the Shield-burg glittered, and the east was
  exceeding clear:
So the eager edges he setteth to the Dwarf-wrought battle-coat
Where the hammered ring-knit collar constraineth the woman's
  throat;
But the sharp Wrath biteth and rendeth, and before it fail the rings,
And, lo, the gleam of the linen, and the light of golden things:
Then he driveth the blue steel onward, and through the skirt, and
  out
Till nought but the rippling linen is wrapping her about;

Then he deems her breath comes quicker and her breast begins to
    heave,
So he turns about the War-flame and rends down either sleeve,
Till her arms lie white in her raiment, and a river of sun-bright hair
Flows free o'er bosom and shoulder and floods the desert bare.

Then a flush cometh over her visage and a sigh up-heaveth her
    breast,
And her eyelids quiver open, and she wakeneth into rest;
Wide-eyed on the dawning she gazeth, too glad to change or smile,
And but little moveth her body, nor speaketh she yet for a while;
And yet kneels Sigurd moveless her wakening speech to heed,
While soft the waves of the daylight o'er the starless heavens speed,
And the gleaming rims of the Shield-burg yet bright and brighter
    grow,
And the thin moon hangeth her horns dead-white in the golden
    glow.

Then she turned and gazed on Sigurd, and her eyes met the
    Volsung's eyes.
And mighty and measureless now did the tide of his love arise,
For their longing had met and mingled, and he knew of her heart
    that she loved,
As she spake unto nothing but him and her lips with the speech-
    flood moved:

'O, what is the thing so mighty that my weary sleep hath torn,
And rent the fallow bondage, and the wan woe over-worn?'

He said: 'The hand of Sigurd and the Sword of Sigmund's son,
And the heart that the Volsungs fashioned this deed for thee have
    done.'

But she said: 'Where then is Odin that laid me here alow?
Long lasteth the grief of the world, and manfolk's tangled woe!'

'He dwelleth above,' said Sigurd, 'but I on the earth abide,
And I came from the Glittering Heath the waves of thy fire to ride.

But therewith the sun rose upward and lightened all the earth,
And the light flashed up to the heavens from the rims of the
glorious girth;
But they twain arose together, and with both her palms outspread,
And bathed in the light returning, she cried aloud and said:

All hail, O Day and thy Sons, and thy kin of the coloured things!
Hail, following Night, and thy Daughter that leadeth thy wavering
wings!
Look down with unangry eyes on us today alive,
And give us the hearts victorious, and the gain for which we strive!
All hail, ye Lords of God-home, and ye Queens of the House of
Gold!
Hail, thou dear Earth that bearest, and thou Wealth of field and
fold!
Give us, your noble children, the glory of wisdom and speech,
And the hearts and the hands of healing, and the mouths and
hands that teach!'

Then they turned and were knit together; and oft and o'er again
They craved, and kissed rejoicing, and their hearts were full and
fain. . . .

iii. HOW SIGURD MET BRYNHILD IN LYMDALE

. . .Now is it the summer-season, and Sigurd rideth the land,
And his hound runs light before him, and his hawk sits light on
his hand,
And all alone on a morning he rides the flowery sward
Betwixt the woodland dwellings and the house of Lymdale's lord;
And he hearkens Greyfell's going as he wends adown the lea,
And his heart for love is craving, and the deeds he deems shall be;
And he hears the Wrath's sheath tinkling as he rides the daisies
down,
And he thinks of his love laid safely in the arms of his renown.
But lo, as he rides the meadows, before him now he sees
A builded burg arising amid the leafy trees,

And a white-walled house on its topmost with a golden roof-
ridge done,
And thereon the clustering dove-kind in the brightness of the sun.
So Sigurd stayed to behold it, for the heart within him laughed,
But e'en then, as the arrow speedeth from the mighty archer's
draught,
Forth fled the falcon unhooded from the hand of Sigurd the King,
And up, and over the tree-boughs he shot with steady wing:
Then the Volsung followed his flight, for he looked to see him fall
On the fluttering folk of the doves, and he cried the backward call
Full oft and over again; but the falcon heeded it nought,
Nor turned to his kingly wrist-perch, nor the folk of the pigeon
sought,
But flew up to a high-built tower, and sat in the window a space,
Crying out like the fowl of Odin when first of the morning they
face,
And then passed through the open casement as an erne to his eyrie
goes.

Much marvelled the Son of Sigmund, and rode to the fruitful close:
For he said: Here a great one dwelleth, though none have told me
thereof,
And he shall give me my falcon, and his fellowship and love.
So he came to the gate of the garth, and forth to the hall-door rode,
And leapt adown from Greyfell, and entered that fair abode;
For full lovely was it fashioned, and great was the pillared hall,
And fair in its hangings were woven the deeds that Kings befall,
And the merry sun went through it and gleamed in gold and horn;
But afield or a-fell are its carles, and none labour there that morn,
And void it is of the maidens, and they weave in the bower aloft,
Or they go in the outer gardens 'twixt the rose and the lily soft:
So saith Sigurd the Volsung, and a door in the corner he spies
With knots of gold fair-carven, and the graver's masteries:
So he lifts the latch and it opens, and he comes to a marble stair,
And aloft by the same he goeth through a tower wrought full fair.
And he comes to a door at its topmost, and lo, a chamber of Kings,
And his falcon there by the window with all unruffled wings.

But a woman sits on the high-seat with gold about her head,
And ruddy rings on her arms, and the grace of her girdle-stead:
And sunlit is her rippled linen, and the green leaves lie at her
    feet,
And e'en as a swan on the billow where the firth and the out-sea
    meet.
On the dark-blue cloth she sitteth, so fair and softly made
Are her limbs by the linen hidden, and so white is she arrayed.
But a web of gold is before her, and therein by her shuttle wrought
The early days of the Volsungs and the war by the sea's rim fought,
And the crowned queen over Sigmund, and the Helper's pillared
    hall,
And the golden babe uplifted to the eyes of duke and thrall:
And there was the slender stripling by the knees of the Dwarf-
    folk's lord,
And the gift of the ancient Gripir, and the forging of the Sword:
And there were the coils of Fafnir, and the hooded threat of death,
And the King by the cooking-fire, and the fowl of the Glittering
    Heath:
And there was the headless King-smith and the golden halls of the
    Worm,
And the laden Greyfell faring through the land of perished storm:
And there was the head of Hindfell, and the flames to the sky-floor
    driven:
And there was the glittering shield-burg, and the fallow bondage
    riven:
And there was the wakening woman and the golden Volsung
    done,
And they twain o'er the earthly kingdoms in the lonely evening
    sun:
And there were fells and forests, and towns and tossing seas,
And the Wrath and the golden Sigurd for ever blent with these,
In the midst of the battle triumphant, in the midst of the war-kings'
    fall,
In the midst of the peace well-conquered, in the midst of the
    praising hall.

There Sigurd stood and marvelled, for he saw his deeds that had
   been,
And his deeds of the days that should be, fair wrought in the
   golden sheen;
And he looked in the face of the woman, and Brynhild's eyes he
   knew,
But still in the door he tarried, and so glad and fair he grew,
That the Gods laughed out in the heavens to see the Volsung's
   seed;
And the breeze blew in from the summer and over Brynhild's
   weed,
Till his heart so swelled with the sweetness that the fair word stayed
   in his mouth,
And a marvel beloved he seemeth, as a ship new-come from the
   south:
And still she longed and beheld him, nor foot nor hand she moved
As she marvelled at her gladness, and her love so well beloved.
But at last through the sounds of summer the voice of Sigurd
   came,
And it seemed as a silver trumpet from the house of the fateful
   fame;
And he spake: 'Hail, lady and queen! hail, fairest of all the earth!
Is it well with the hap of thy life-days, and thy kin and the house of
   thy birth?'. . . .

The Burghers' Battle

Thick rise the spear-shafts o'er the land
That erst the harvest bore;
The sword is heavy in the hand,
And we return no more.
The light wind waves the Ruddy Fox,
Our banner of the war,
And ripples in the Running Ox,
And we return no more.

Across our stubble acres now
The teams go four and four;
But out-worn elders guide the plough,
And we return no more.
And now the women heavy-eyed
Turn through the open door
From gazing down the highway wide,
Where we return no more.
The shadows of the fruited close
Dapple the feast-hall floor;
There lie our dogs and dream and doze,
And we return no more.
Down from the minster tower to-day
Fall the soft chimes of yore
Amidst the chattering jackdaws' play:
And we return no more.
But underneath the streets are still;
Noon, and the market's o'er!
Back go the goodwives o'er the hill;
For we return no more.
What merchant to our gates shall come?
What wise man bring us lore?
What abbot ride away to Rome,
Now we return no more?
What mayor shall rule the hall we built?
Whose scarlet sweep the floor?
What judge shall doom the robber's guilt,
Now we return no more?
New houses in the street shall rise
Where builded we before,
Of other stone wrought otherwise;
For we return no more.
And crops shall cover field and hill
Unlike what once they bore,
And all be done without our will,
Now we return no more.
Look up! the arrows streak the sky,
The horns of battle roar;

The long spears lower and draw nigh,
And we return no more.
Remember how beside the wain,
We spoke the word of war,
And sowed this harvest of the plain,
And we return no more.
Lay spears about the Ruddy Fox !
The days of old are o'er ;
Heave sword about the Running Ox !
For we return no more.

The Hall and the Wood

'Twas in the water-dwindling tide
When July days were done,
Sir Rafe of Greenhowes 'gan to ride
In the earliest of the sun.

He left the white-walled burg behind,
He rode amidst the wheat.
The westland-gotten wind blew kind
Across the acres sweet.

Then rose his heart and cleared his brow,
And slow he rode the way :
'As then it was, so is it now,
Not all hath worn away.'

So came he to the long green lane
That leadeth to the ford,
And saw the sickle by the wain
Shine bright as any sword.

The brown carles stayed 'twixt draught and draught,
And murmuring, stood aloof,
But one spake out when he had laughed:
'God bless the Green-wood Roof!'

Then o'er the ford and up he fared:
And lo the happy hills!
And the mountain-dale by summer cleared,
That oft the winter fills.

Then forth he rode by Peter's gate,
And smiled and said aloud:
'No more a day doth the Prior wait;
White stands the tower and proud.'

There leaned a knight on the gateway side
In armour white and wan,
And after the heels of the horse he cried,
'God keep the hunted man!'

Then quoth Sir Rafe, 'Amen, amen!'
For he deemed the word was good;
But never a while he lingered then
Till he reached the Nether Wood.

He rode by ash, he rode by oak,
He rode the thicket round,
And heard no woodman strike a stroke,
No wandering wife he found.

He rode the wet, he rode the dry,
He rode the grassy glade:
At Wood-end yet the sun was high,
And his heart was unafraid.

There on the bent his rein he drew,
And looked o'er field and fold,
O'er all the merry meads he knew
Beneath the mountains old.

He gazed across to the Good Green Howe
As he smelt the sun-warmed sward;
Then his face grew pale from chin to brow,
And he cried, 'God save the sword!'

For there beyond the winding way,
Above the orchards green,
Stood up the ancient gables grey
With ne'er a roof between.

His naked blade in hand he had,
O'er rough and smooth he rode,
Till he stood where once his heart was glad
Amidst his old abode.

Across the hearth a tie-beam lay
Unmoved a weary while.
The flame that clomb the ashlar grey
Had burned it red as tile.

The sparrows bickering on the floor
Fled at his entering in;
The swift flew past the empty door
His winged meat to win.

Red apples from the tall old tree
O'er the wall's rent were shed.
Thence oft, a little lad, would he
Look down upon the lead.

There turned the cheeping chaffinch now
And feared no birding child;
Through the shot-window thrust a bough
Of garden-rose run wild.

He looked to right, he looked to left,
And down to the cold grey hearth,
Where lay an axe with half burned heft
Amidst the ashen dearth.

He caught it up and cast it wide
Against the gable wall;
Then to the daïs did he stride,
O'er beam and bench and all.

Amidst there yet the high-seat stood,
Where erst his sires had sat;
And the mighty board of oaken wood,
The fire had stayed thereat.

Then through the red wrath of his eyne
He saw a sheathed sword,
Laid thwart that wasted field of wine,
Amidmost of the board.

And by the hilts a slug-horn lay,
And therebeside a scroll,
He caught it up and turned away
From the lea-land of the bowl.

Then with the sobbing grief he strove,
For he saw his name thereon;
And the heart within his breast uphove
As the pen's tale now he won.

'O Rafe, my love of long ago!
Draw forth thy father's blade,
And blow the horn for friend and foe,
And the good green-wood to aid!'

He turned and took the slug-horn up,
And set it to his mouth,
And o'er that meadow of the cup
Blew east and west and south.

He drew the sword from out the sheath
And shook the fallow brand;
And there a while with bated breath,
And hearkening ear did stand.

Him-seemed the horn's voice he might hear —
Or the wind that blew o'er all.
Him-seemed that footsteps drew anear —
Or the boughs shook round the hall.

Him-seemed he heard a voice he knew —
Or a dream of while agone.
Him-seemed bright raiment towards him drew —
Or bright the sun-set shone.

She stood before him face to face,
With the sun-beam thwart her hand,
As on the gold of the Holy Place
The painted angels stand.

With many a kiss she closed his eyes;
She kissed him cheek and chin:
E'en so in the painted Paradise
Are Earth's folk welcomed in.

There in the door the green-coats stood,
O'er the bows went up the cry,
'O welcome, Rafe, to the free green-wood,
With us to live and die.'

It was bill and bow by the high-seat stood,
And they cried above the bows,
'Now welcome, Rafe, to the good green-wood,
And welcome Kate the Rose!'

White, white in the moon is the woodland plash,
White is the woodland glade,
Forth wend those twain, from oak to ash,
With light hearts unafraid.

The summer moon high o'er the hill,
All silver-white is she,
And Sir Rafe's good men with bow and bill,
They go by two and three.

In the fair green-wood where lurks no fear,
Where the King's writ runneth not,
There dwell they, friends and fellows dear,
While summer days are hot.

And when the leaf from the oak-tree falls,
And winds blow rough and strong,
With the carles of the woodland thorps and halls
They dwell, and fear no wrong.

And there the merry yule they make,
And see the winter wane,
And fain are they for true-love's sake,
And the folk thereby are fain.

For the ploughing carle and the straying herd
Flee never for Sir Rafe:
No barefoot maiden wends afeard,
And she deems the thicket safe.

But sore adread do the chapmen ride;
Wide round the wood they go;
And the judge and the sergeants wander wide,
Lest they plead before the bow.

Well learned and wise is Sir Rafe's good sword,
And straight the arrows fly,
And they find the coat of many a lord,
And the crest that rideth high.

Mother and Son

Now sleeps the land of houses, and dead night holds the street,
And there thou liest, my baby, and sleepest soft and sweet;
My man is away for awhile, but safe and alone we lie;
And none heareth thy breath but thy mother, and the moon looking
    down from the sky
On the weary waste of the town, as it looked on the grass-edged
    road
Still warm with yesterday's sun, when I left my old abode,
Hand in hand with my love, that night of all nights in the year;
When the river of love o'erflowed and drowned all doubt and fear,
And we two were alone in the world, and once, if never again,
We knew of the secret of earth and the tale of its labour and pain.

Lo amidst London I lift thee, and how little and light thou art,
And thou without hope or fear, thou fear and hope of my heart!
Lo here thy body beginning, O son, and thy soul and thy life;
But how will it be if thou livest, and enterest into the strife,
And in love we dwell together when the man is grown in thee,
When thy sweet speech I shall hearken, and yet 'twixt thee and me
Shall rise that wall of distance, that round each other doth grow,
And maketh it hard and bitter each other's thought to know?

Now, therefore, while yet thou art little and hast no thought of
    thine own,
I will tell thee a word of the world, of the hope whence thou hast
    grown,
Of the love that once begat thee, of the sorrow that hath made
Thy little heart of hunger, and thy hands on my bosom laid.
Then mayst thou remember hereafter, as whiles when people say
All this hath happened before in the life of another day;
So mayst thou dimly remember this tale of thy mother's voice,
As oft in the calm of dawning I have heard the birds rejoice,
As oft I have heard the storm-wind go moaning through the wood,
And I knew that earth was speaking, and the mother's voice was
    good.

Now, to thee alone will I tell it that thy mother's body is fair,
In the guise of the country maidens who play with the sun and
the air,
Who have stood in the row of the reapers in the August afternoon,
Who have sat by the frozen water in the highday of the moon,
When the lights of the Christmas feasting were dead in the house
on the hill,
And the wild geese gone to the salt marsh had left the winter
still.
Yea, I am fair, my firstling; if thou couldst but remember me!
The hair that thy small hand clutcheth is a goodly sight to see;
I am true, but my face is a snare; soft and deep are my eyes,
And they seem for men's beguiling fulfilled with the dreams of
the wise.
Kind are my lips, and they look as though my soul had learned
Deep things I have never heard of. My face and my hands are
burned
By the lovely sun of the acres; three months of London-town
And thy birth-bed have bleached them indeed — 'But lo, where
the edge of the gown'
(So said thy father) is parting the wrist that is white as the curd
From the brown of the hands that I love, bright as the wing of
a bird.'

Such is thy mother, O firstling, yet strong as the maidens of old,
Whose spears and whose swords were the warders of homestead,
of field and of fold.
Oft were my feet on the highway, often they wearied the grass;
From dusk unto dusk of the summer three times in a week would
I pass
To the downs from the house on the river through the waves of the
blossoming corn.
Fair then I lay down in the even, and fresh I arose on the morn,
And scarce in the noon was I weary. Ah, son, in the days of thy
strife,
If thy soul could harbour a dream of the blossom of my life!
It would be as sunlit meadows beheld from a tossing sea,
And thy soul should look on a vision of the peace that is to be.

136

Yet, yet the tears on my cheek! And what is this doth move
My heart to thy heart, beloved, save the flood of yearning love?
For fair and fierce is thy father, and soft and strange are his eyes
That look on the days that shall be with the hope of the brave and
    the wise.
It was many a day that we laughed as over the meadows we walked,
And many a day I hearkened and the pictures came as he talked;
It was many a day that we longed, and we lingered late at eve
Ere speech from speech was sundered, and my hand his hand could
    leave.
Then I wept when I was alone, and I longed till the daylight came;
And down the stairs I stole, and there was our housekeeping dame
(No mother of me, the foundling) kindling the fire betimes
Ere the haymaking folk went forth to the meadows down by the
    limes;
All things I saw at a glance; the quickening fire-tongues leapt
Through the crackling heap of sticks, and the sweet smoke up
    from it crept,
And close to the very hearth the low sun flooded the floor,
And the cat and her kittens played in the sun by the open door.
The garden was fair in the morning, and there in the road he stood
Beyond the crimson daisies and the bush of southernwood.
Then side by side together through the grey-walled place we went,
And O the fear departed, and the rest and sweet content!

Son, sorrow and wisdom he taught me, and sore I grieved and
    learned
As we twain grew into one; and the heart within me burned
With the very hopes of his heart. Ah, son, it is piteous,
But never again in my life shall I dare to speak to thee thus;
So may these lonely words about thee creep and cling,
These words of the lonely night in the days of our wayfaring.
Many a child of woman to-night is born in the town,
The desert of folly and wrong; and of what and whence are they
    grown?
Many and many an one of wont and use is born;
For a husband is taken to bed as a hat or a ribbon is worn.
Prudence begets her thousands: 'Good is a housekeeper's life,

So shall I sell my body that I may be matron and wife.'
'And I shall endure foul wedlock and bear the children of need.'
Some are there born of hate — many the children of greed.
'I, I too can be wedded, though thou my love hast got.'
'I am fair and hard of heart, and riches shall be my lot.'
And all these are the good and the happy, on whom the world
    dawns fair.
O son, when wilt thou learn of those that are born of despair,
As the fabled mud of the Nile that quickens under the sun
With a growth of creeping things, half dead when just begun?
E'en such is the care of Nature that man should never die,
Though she breed of the fools of the earth, and the dregs of the
    city sty.
But thou, O son, O son, of very love wert born,
When our hope fulfilled bred hope, and fear was a folly outworn;
On the eve of the toil and the battle all sorrow and grief we weighed,
We hoped and we were not ashamed, we knew and we were not
    afraid.

Now waneth the night and the moon — ah, son, it is piteous
That never again in my life shall I dare to speak to thee thus.
But sure from the wise and the simple shall the mighty come to
    birth;
And fair were my fate, beloved, if I be yet on the earth
When the world is awaken at last, and from mouth to mouth they
    tell
Of thy love and thy deeds and thy valour, and thy hope that nought
    can quell.

A Death Song

What cometh here from west to east awending?
And who are these, the marchers stern and slow?
We bear the message that the rich are sending
Aback to those who bade them wake and know.
Not one, not one, nor thousands must they slay,
But one and all if they would dusk the day.

We asked them for a life of toilsome earning,
They bade us bide their leisure for our bread;
We craved to speak to tell our woeful learning:
We come back speechless, bearing back our dead.
Not one, not one, nor thousands must they slay,
But one and all if they would dusk the day.

They will not learn; they have no ears to hearken.
They turn their faces from the eyes of fate;
Their gay-lit halls shut out the skies that darken.
But, lo! this dead man knocking at the gate.
Not one, not one, nor thousands must they slay,
But one and all if they would dusk the day.

Here lies the sign that we shall break our prison;
Amidst the storm he won a prisoner's rest;
But in the cloudy dawn the sun arisen
Brings us our day of work to win the best.
Not one, not one, nor thousands must they slay,
But one and all if they would dusk the day.

The God of the Poor

There was a lord that hight Maltete,
Among great lords he was right great,
On poor folk trod he like the dirt,
None but God might do him hurt.
Deus est Deus pauperum.

139

With a grace of prayers sung loud and late
Many a widow's house he ate;
Many a poor knight at his hands
Lost his house and narrow lands.
Deus est Deus pauperum.

He burnt the harvests many a time,
He made fair houses heaps of lime;
Whatso man loved wife or maid
Of Evil-head was sore afraid.
Deus est Deus pauperum.

He slew good men and spared the bad;
Too long a day the foul dog had,
E'en as all dogs will have their day;
But God is as strong as man, I say.
Deus est Deus pauperum.

For a valiant knight, men called Boncœur,
Had hope he should not long endure,
And gathered to him much good folk,
Hardy hearts to break the yoke.
Deus est Deus pauperum.

But Boncœur deemed it would be vain
To strive his guarded house to gain;
Therefore, within a little while,
He set himself to work by guile.
Deus est Deus pauperum.

He knew that Maltete loved right well
Red gold and heavy. If from hell
The Devil had cried, 'Take this gold cup,'
Down had he gone to fetch it up.
Deus est Deus pauperum.

Twenty poor men's lives were nought
To him, beside a ring well wrought.
The pommel of his hunting-knife
Was worth ten times a poor man's life.
Deus est Deus pauperum.

A squire new-come from over-sea
Boncœur called to him privily,
And when he knew his lord's intent,
Clad like a churl therefrom he went.
Deus est Deus pauperum.

But when he came where dwelt Maltete,
With few words did he pass the gate,
For Maltete built him walls anew,
And, wageless, folk from field he drew.
Deus est Deus pauperum.

Now passed the squire through this and that,
Till he came to where Sir Maltete sat,
And over red wine wagged his beard:
Then spoke the squire as one afeard.
Deus est Deus pauperum.

'Lord, give me grace, for privily
I have a little word for thee.'
'Speak out,' said Maltete, 'have no fear,
For how can thy life to thee be dear?'
Deus est Deus pauperum.

'Such an one I know,' he said,
'Who hideth store of money red.'
Maltete grinned at him cruelly:
'Thou florin-maker, come anigh.'
Deus est Deus pauperum.

'E'en such as thou once preached of gold,
And showed me lies in books full old,
Nought gat I but evil brass,
Therefore came he to the worser pass.'
Deus est Deus pauperum.

'Hast thou will to see his skin?
I keep my heaviest marks therein,
For since nought else of wealth had he,
I deemed full well he owed it me.'
Deus est Deus pauperum.

'Nought know I of philosophy,'
The other said, 'nor do I lie.
Before the moon begins to shine,
May all this heap of gold be thine.'
Deus est Deus pauperum.

'Ten leagues from this a man there is,
Who seemeth to know but little bliss,
And yet full many a pound of gold
A dry well nigh his house doth hold.'
Deus est Deus pauperum.

'John-a-Wood is he called, fair lord,
Nor know I whence he hath this hoard.'
Then Maltete said, 'As God made me,
A wizard over-bold is he!'
Deus est Deus pauperum.

'It were a good deed, as I am a knight,
To burn him in a fire bright;
This John-a-Wood shall surely die,
And his gold in my strong chest shall lie.'
Deus est Deus pauperum.

'This very night, I make mine avow,
The truth of this mine eyes shall know.'
Then spoke an old knight in the hall,
'Who knoweth what things may befall?'
Deus est Deus pauperum.

'I rede thee go with a great rout,
For thy foes they ride thick about.'
'Thou and the devil may keep my foes,
Thou redest me this gold to lose.'
Deus est Deus pauperum.

'I shall go with but some four or five,
So shall I take my thief alive.
For if a great rout he shall see,
Will he not hide his wealth from me?'
Deus est Deus pauperum.

The old knight muttered under his breath,
'Then mayhap ye shall but ride to death.'
But Maltete turned him quickly round,
'Bind me this grey-beard under ground!'
Deus est Deus pauperum.

'Because ye are old, ye think to jape.
Take heed, ye shall not long escape.
When I come back safe, old carle, perdie,
Thine head shall brush the linden-tree.'
Deus est Deus pauperum.

Therewith he rode with his five men,
And Boncœur's spy, for good leagues ten,
Until they left the beaten way,
And dusk it grew at end of day.
Deus est Deus pauperum.

There, in a clearing of the wood,
Was John's house, neither fair nor good.
In a ragged plot his house anigh,
Thin coleworts grew but wretchedly.
Deus est Deus pauperum.

John-a-Wood in his doorway sat,
Turning over this and that,
And chiefly how he best might thrive,
For he had will enough to live.
Deus est Deus pauperum.

Green coleworts from a wooden bowl
He ate; but careful was his soul,
For if he saw another day,
Thenceforth was he in Boncœur's pay.
Deus est Deus pauperum.

So when he saw how Maltete came,
He said, 'Beginneth now the game!'
And in the doorway did he stand
Trembling, with hand joined fast to hand.
Deus est Deus pauperum.

When Maltete did this carle behold
Somewhat he doubted of his gold,
But cried out, 'Where is now thy store
Thou hast through books of wicked lore?'
Deus est Deus pauperum.

Then said the poor man, right humbly,
'Fair lord, this was not made by me,
I found it in mine own dry well,
And had a mind thy grace to tell.
Deus est Deus pauperum.

'Therefrom, my lord, a cup I took
This day, that thou thereon mightst look,
And know me to be leal and true,'
And from his coat the cup he drew.
Deus est Deus pauperum.

Then Maltete took it in his hand,
Nor knew he aught that it used to stand
On Boncœur's cupboard many a day.
'Go on,' he said, 'and show the way.'
Deus est Deus pauperum.

'Give me thy gold, and thou shalt live,
Yea, in my house thou well mayst thrive.'
John turned about and 'gan to go
Unto the wood with footsteps slow.
Deus est Deus pauperum.

But as they passed by John's woodstack,
Growled Maltete, 'Nothing now doth lack
Wherewith to light a merry fire,
And give my wizard all his hire.'
Deus est Deus pauperum.

The western sky was red as blood,
Darker grew the oaken-wood;
'Thief and carle, where are ye gone?
Why are we in the wood alone?
Deus est Deus pauperum.

'What is the sound of this mighty horn?
Ah, God! that ever I was born!
The basnets flash from tree to tree;
Show me, thou Christ, the way to flee!'
Deus est Deus pauperum.

Boncœur it was with fifty men;
Maltete was but one to ten,
And his own folk prayed for grace,
With empty hands in that lone place.
Deus est Deus pauperum.

'Grace shall ye have,' Boncœur said,
'All of you but Evil-head.'
Lowly could that great lord be,
Who could pray so well as he?
Deus est Deus pauperum.

Then could Maltete howl and cry,
Little will he had to die.
Soft was his speech, now it was late,
But who had will to save Maltete?
Deus est Deus pauperum.

They brought him to the house again,
And toward the road he looked in vain.
Lonely and bare was the great highway,
Under the gathering moonlight grey.
Deus est Deus pauperum.

They took off his gilt basnet,
That he should die there was no let;
They took off his coat of steel,
A damned man he well might feel.
Deus est Deus pauperum.

'Will ye all be rich as kings,
Lacking naught of all good things?'
'Nothing do we lack this eve;
When thou art dead, how can we grieve?'
Deus est Deus pauperum.

'Let me drink water ere I die,
None henceforth comes my lips anigh.'
They brought it him in that bowl of wood.
He said, 'This is but poor men's blood!'
Deus est Deus pauperum.

They brought it him in the cup of gold.
He said, 'The women I have sold
Have wept it full of salt for me;
I shall die gaping thirstily.'
Deus est Deus pauperum.

On the threshold of that poor homestead
They smote off his evil head;
They set it high on a great spear,
And rode away with merry cheer.
Deus est Deus pauperum.

At the dawn, in lordly state,
They rode to Maltete's castle-gate.
'Whoso willeth laud to win,
Make haste to let your masters in!'
Deus est Deus pauperum.

Forthwith opened they the gate,
No man was sorry for Maltete.
Boncœur conquered all his lands,
A good knight was he of his hands.
Deus est Deus pauperum.

Good men he loved, and hated bad;
Joyful days and sweet he had;
Good deeds did he plenteously;
Beneath him folk lived frank and free.
Deus est Deus pauperum.

He lived long, with merry days;
None said aught of him but praise.
God on him have full mercy;
A good knight merciful was he.
Deus est Deus pauperum.

The great lord, called Maltete, is dead;
Grass grows above his feet and head,
And a holly-bush grows up between
His rib-bones gotten white and clean.
Deus est Deus pauperum.

A carle's sheep-dog certainly
Is a mightier thing than he.
Till London-bridge shall cross the Nen,
Take we heed of such-like men.
Deus est Deus pauperum.

The Folk-Mote by the River

It was up in the morn we rose betimes
From the hall-floor hard by the row of limes.

It was but John the Red and I,
And we were the brethren of Gregory;

And Gregory the Wright was one
Of the valiant men beneath the sun,

And what he bade us that we did
For ne'er he kept his counsel hid.

So out we went, and the clattering latch
Woke up the swallows under the thatch.

It was dark in the porch, but our scythes we felt,
And thrust the whetstone under the belt.

148

Through the cold garden boughs we went
Where the tumbling roses shed their scent.

Then out a-gates and away we strode
O'er the dewy straws on the dusty road,

And there was the mead by the town-reeve's close
Where the hedge was sweet with the wilding rose.

Then into the mowing grass we went
Ere the very last of the night was spent.

Young was the moon, and he was gone,
So we whet our scythes by the stars alone:

But or ever the long blades felt the hay
Afar in the East the dawn was grey.

Or ever we struck our earliest stroke
The thrush in the hawthorn-bush awoke.

While yet the bloom of the swathe was dim
The blackbird's bill had answered him.

Ere half of the road to the river was shorn
The sunbeam smote the twisted thorn.

Now wide was the way 'twixt the standing grass
For the townsfolk unto the mote to pass,

And so when all our work was done
We sat to breakfast in the sun,

While down in the stream the dragon-fly
'Twixt the quivering rushes flickered by;

And though our knives shone sharp and white
The swift bleak heeded not the sight.

So when the bread was done away
We looked along the new-shorn hay,

And heard the voice of the gathering-horn
Come over the garden and the corn;

For the wind was in the blossoming wheat
And drave the bees in the lime-boughs sweet.

Then loud was the horn's voice drawing near,
And it hid the talk of the prattling weir.

And now was the horn on the pathway wide
That we had shorn to the river-side.

So up we stood, and wide around
We sheared a space by the Elders' Mound;

And at the feet thereof it was
That highest grew the June-tide grass;

And over all the mound it grew
With clover blent, and dark of hue.

But never aught of the Elders' Hay
To rick or barn was borne away.

But it was bound and burned to ash
In the barren close by the reedy plash.

For 'neath that mound the valiant dead
Lay hearkening words of valiance said

When wise men stood on the Elders' Mound,
And the swords were shining bright around.

And now we saw the banners borne
On the first of the way that we had shorn;
So we laid the scythe upon the sward
And girt us to the battle-sword.

For after the banners well we knew
Were the Freemen wending two and two.

There then that highway of the scythe
With many a hue was brave and blythe.

And first below the Silver Chief
Upon the green was the golden sheaf.

And on the next that went by it
The White Hart in the Park did sit.

Then on the red the White Wings flew,
And on the White was the Cloud-fleck blue.

Last went the Anchor of the Wrights
Beside the Ship of the Faring-Knights.

Then thronged the folk the June-tide field
With naked sword and painted shield,

Till they came adown to the river-side,
And there by the mound did they abide.

Now when the swords stood thick and white
As the mace reeds stand in the streamless bight,

There rose a man on the mound alone
And over his head was the grey mail done.

When over the new-shorn place of the field
Was nought but the steel hood and the shield.

The face on the mound shone ruddy and hale,
But the hoar hair showed from the hoary mail.

And there rose a hand by the ruddy face
And shook a sword o'er the peopled place.

And there came a voice from the mound and said :
'O sons, the days of my youth are dead,

And gone are the faces I have known
In the street and the booths of the goodly town.

O sons, full many a flock have I seen
Feed down this water-girdled green.

Full many a herd of long-horned neat
Have I seen 'twixt water-side and wheat.

Here by this water-side full oft
Have I heaved the flowery hay aloft.

And oft this water-side anigh
Have I bowed adown the wheat-stalks high.

And yet meseems I live and learn
And lore of younglings yet must earn.

For tell me, children, whose are these
Fair meadows of the June's increase?

Whose are these flocks and whose the neat,
And whose the acres of the wheat?'

Scarce did we hear his latest word,
On the wide shield so rang the sword.

So rang the sword upon the shield
That the lark was hushed above the field.

Then sank the shouts and again we heard
The old voice come from the hoary beard :

'Yea, whose are yonder gables then,
And whose the holy hearths of men?
Whose are the prattling children there,
And whose the sunburnt maids and fair?

Whose thralls are ye, hereby that stand,
Bearing the freeman's sword in hand?'

As glitters the sun in the rain-washed grass,
So in the tossing swords it was;

As the thunder rattles along and adown
E'en so was the voice of the weaponed town.

And there was the steel of the old man's sword,
And there was his hollow voice, and his word:

'Many men, many minds, the old saw saith,
Though hereof ye be sure as death.

For what spake the herald yestermorn
But this, that ye were thrall-folk born;

That the lord that owneth all and some
Would send his men to fetch us home

Betwixt the haysel, and the tide
When they shear the corn in the country-side?

O children, Who was the lord? ye say,
What prayer to him did our fathers pray?

Did they hold out hands his gyves to bear?
Did their knees his high hall's pavement wear?

Is his house built up in heaven aloft?
Doth he make the sun rise oft and oft?

Doth he hold the rain in his hollow hand?
Hath he cleft this water through the land?

Or doth he stay the summer-tide,
And make the winter days abide?

O children, Who is the lord? ye say,
Have we heard his name before to-day?

O children, if his name I know,
He hight Earl Hugh of the Shivering Low:

For that herald bore on back and breast
The Black Burg under the Eagle's Nest.'

As the voice of the winter wind that tears
At the eaves of the thatch and its emptied ears,

E'en so was the voice of laughter and scorn
By the water-side in the mead new-shorn;

And over the garden and the wheat
Went the voice of women shrilly-sweet.

But now by the hoary elder stood
A carle in raiment red as blood.

Red was his weed and his glaive was white,
And there stood Gregory the Wright.

So he spake in a voice was loud and strong:
'Young is the day though the road is long;

There is time if we tarry nought at all
For the kiss in the porch and the meat in the hall.

And safe shall our maidens sit at home
For the foe by the way we wend must come.

Through the three Lavers shall we go
And raise them all against the foe.

Then shall we wend the Downland ways,
And all the shepherd spearmen raise.

To Cheaping Raynes shall we come adown
And gather the bowmen of the town;

And Greenstead next we come unto
Wherein are all folk good and true.

When we come our ways to the Outer Wood
We shall be an host both great and good;

Yea when we come to the open field
There shall be a many under shield.

And maybe Earl Hugh shall lie alow
And yet to the house of Heaven shall go.

But we shall dwell in the land we love
And grudge no hallow Heaven above.

Come ye, who think the time o'er long
Till we have slain the word of wrong!

Come ye who deem the life of fear
On this last day hath drawn o'er near!

Come after me upon the road
That leadeth to the Erne's abode.'

Down then he leapt from off the mound
And back drew they that were around

Till he was foremost of all those
Betwixt the river and the close.

And uprose shouts both glad and strong
As followed after all the throng;

And overhead the banners flapped,
As we went on our ways to all that happed.

The fields before the Shivering Low
Of many a grief of manfolk know;

There may the autumn acres tell
Of how men met, and what befell.

The Black Burg under the Eagle's nest
Shall tell the tale as it liketh best.

And sooth it is that the River-land
Lacks many an autumn-gathering hand.

And there are troth-plight maids unwed
Shall deem awhile that love is dead;

And babes there are to men shall grow
Nor ever the face of their fathers know.

And yet in the Land by the River-side
Doth never a thrall or an earl's man bide;

For Hugh the Earl of might and mirth
Hath left the merry days of Earth;

And we live on in the land we love,
And grudge no hallow Heaven above.

[*Fair is the World*]

Fair is the world, now autumn's wearing,
And the sluggard sun lies long abed;
Sweet are the days, now winter's nearing,
And all winds feign that the wind is dead.

Dumb is the hedge where the crabs hang yellow,
Bright as the blossoms of the spring;
Dumb is the close where the pears grow mellow,
And none but the dauntless redbreasts sing.

Fair was the spring, but amidst his greening
Grey were the days of the hidden sun;
Fair was the summer, but overweening,
So soon his o'er-sweet days were done.

Come then, love, for peace is upon us,
Far off is failing, and far is fear,
Here where the rest in the end hath won us,
In the garnering tide of the happy year.

Come from the grey old house by the water,
Where, far from the lips of the hungry sea,
Green groweth the grass o'er the field of the slaughter,
And all is a tale for thee and me.

For the Bed at Kelmscott

The wind's on the wold
And the night is a-cold,
And Thames runs chill
Twixt mead and hill,
But kind and dear
Is the old house here,
And my heart is warm
Midst winter's harm.
Rest, then and rest,
And think of the best
Twixt summer and spring
When all birds sing
In the town of the tree,
And ye lie in me

157

But scarce dare move
Lest earth and its love
Should fade away
Ere the full of the day.

I am old and have seen
Many things that have been,
Both grief and peace,
And wane and increase.
No tale I tell
Of ill or well,
But this I say,
Night treadeth on day,
And for worst and best
Right good is rest.

Index of First Lines